A HEALING CONVERSATION

A HEALING CONVERSATION

How Healing Happens

Neville Symington

KARNAC
LONDON   NEW YORK

First published in 2006 by
H. Karnac (Books) Ltd.
6 Pembroke Buildings, London NW10 6RE

British Library Cataloguing in Publication Data

A C.I.P. for this book is available from the British Library

ISBN: 1-85575-359-6

Edited, designed, and produced by Communication Crafts

Printed in Great Britain

www.karnacbooks.com

For Shahid Najeeb
In Gratitude

CONTENTS

PREFACE

A conversation that heals

We take it for granted that we can solve a problem by going to visit a psychoanalyst, a psychotherapist, or a counsellor; but how is someone able to solve a problem by going to visit such a professional? Or, for that matter, how can an intimate conversation have the power to heal an emotional problem? Or can it? The author of this book assumes that it can, but it is a very big assumption, and this book's purpose is to try to understand just how such a conversation is able to relieve a person's emotional suffering.

This question has interested me for some time, so in the year 2004 I gave six successive lectures on the subject in Sydney to an audience made up mostly of clinicians, though there were some people who were just interested in the subject, with no professional stake in it. Then, on the last weekend of February 2005, I gave the whole lot in Melbourne. This book is based upon these lectures, but there is more text here than there could be in the lectures, and there are also many more quotations in the book. A reader can always skip a quotation, but a person in the audience has to sit and listen. The text here still reflects the lecture style. It has at times been recommended that I alter the lecture format, but readers have regularly told me that they can feel they are in the room listening, and they like that. I have followed their recommendation and left the lecture mode undisturbed.

A HEALING CONVERSATION

CHAPTER ONE

The question:
an intellectual solution

The question: *How is it that someone who has a problem is able to resolve it through conversation with another?*

"I remind myself of the old advice that the doctrines which best repay critical examination are those which for the longest period have remained unquestioned."

Alfred North Whitehead [1942, p. 207]

This is the question that I want to try to resolve here. It is a question that is so basic that we all take it for granted. Yet I believe that if we attempt to seek an answer to this very basic question, the very attempt can open up great avenues of new thinking and surprising perspectives. I do not know the answer to this question. I am out in the bush at night. I have a torch in my hand, and I point the beam out into the dark. I am stumbling. I cannot see my way very easily; I am surrounded by blackness. I need some support, or else I might fall.

Now I need to explain something about my style of presentation. I put forward various propositions on which I base other statements that I make. These propositions are what I think, and

I usually put what I have to say with certainty. I tend not to keep putting in phrases like "I might be wrong, of course" or "Maybe" or "This is what I think at the moment" and so on. Such phrases detract from the object that one is attempting to observe and understand. A constant breast-beating is tiresome and takes attention away from the object of scrutiny. So the situation is that I feel that the propositions I put forward are right but I *know* that this cannot be so. If I am alive in ten years' time I am certain that I shall judge that some perspectives are either wrong or inadequate. So I *feel* what I am going to say is right, but at the same time I *know* that cannot be so. However, you have full licence to be angry when you hear me assert a proposition with certainty. I do not want to diminish your freedom when that angry feeling wells up in you, but I would be very pleased if you converted that raw feeling into a potent criticism. If you do this, then we shall all learn. There is one other thing I want to mention: that I have given more quotes here than I usually do. My reason is that these are always quotes that have stimulated new thoughts and perspectives in me and may do the same for others too, and some of you may want to follow up on these quotes and read the original works from which they are taken. So let us get going.

* * *

The whole of psychoanalysis and psychotherapy is based upon the assumption that it is possible for one person to resolve a problem through talking to another. If this were not the case, then that huge industry that encompasses psychotherapists in their offices honeycombed in crevices, skyscrapers, and unsuspecting terraces of all modern cities in the Western world would collapse, like the Twin Towers, into a heap of miserable rubble. Now I am basing myself on the truth of this assumption: that through communication with another person I am able to solve emotional problems in myself. I am, however, in dark ignorance of why this should be so. The lectures on which this book is based are the first probes into the darkness in the hope of finding the first inklings of an answer to this question. Heaven knows if by the end of them we shall be any closer to satisfying this quest. If any of you know and think it is obvious why a problem can be solved by communicating with another, then you are in the wrong place, and you can leave without giving any offence.

So let us look at the question. So someone has a problem. What do we mean by this? Can I put this into any other words? I think back to when I first approached a psychoanalyst. What impelled me to do so? Is it that I had a problem? That sounds too pale, too intellectual, too tepid an expression. I was suffering. Ah, yes, that is closer to how it was. I was in distress. Even that is too mild. I was in agony, and I had a dim sense that what I needed was to communicate deeply with another person. I remember very well that when I made that decision, I felt through that very decision that I was doing something personal. That very choice laid down something in my personality that has always remained with me. Kierkegaard has given lucid expression to this:

> I would say that the experience of choosing imparts to a man's nature a solemnity, a quiet dignity, which never is entirely lost. There are many who set great store upon having seen one or another distinguished world-historical personality face to face.
>
> This impression they never forget, it has given to their souls an ideal picture which ennobles their nature; and yet such an instant, however significant, is nothing in comparison with the instant of choice. . . . Then has the soul beheld the loftiest sight that mortal eye can see and which can never be forgotten, then the personality receives the accolade of knighthood which ennobles it for an eternity. [1971, p. 181]

There was a freedom in it that was liberating. I inhabited an environment that was hostile to psychoanalysis, that viewed it with suspicion. Rather than be controlled by this attitude, I had decided to make contact with myself. I was going to engage in a close association with another person. I use the phrase "another person" somewhat nonchalantly and, in fact, misguidedly. The phrase suggests that I was a person: but was I? There is a very crucial difference between a statement that I make that is personal and one that is robotic. So I think the situation was that there was a something in me struggling to become a person, but it was smothered behind a whole quantum of stuff that I had just ingested. That something struggling to become a person was smothered beneath a heavy weight of undigested debris. So there was an inchoate sense that I needed to communicate with someone who was a person. But who? I had heard of some shadowy specialists called *psycho-analysts* and that perhaps one of them might understand what I was wanting to communicate. Of course it is totally absurd to think that a whole professional grouping could have the understand-ing I needed: in fact, the first one whom I approached and with whom I had an analytic treatment for three years did not have the understanding I required, and I therefore took my leave of him. Understanding of the kind I needed was a rare gem. However, I had some idea that I would be more likely to find it among that group that styled themselves *psychoanalysts* than among lawyers, accountants, or personnel managers, or, for that matter, doctors, social workers, or counsellors. I had a vague notion that it was among these professionals calling themselves *psychoanalysts* that I was most likely to find an individual who would help me to alleviate a dire anguish.

Now I did not know the reason for my distress. If it had been absolutely clear to me why I was troubled, then I would not have wanted or even thought of going to speak to someone. If I had known what was distressing me, then I would have acted accord-ing to my knowledge. I was far too proud to go seeking help unless I was desperate about the cloud of unknowing that surrounded me. So I think an inherent aspect of my distress was precisely that I did not know the reason for it.

* * *

A new friend of mine decided to uproot his family and interrupt his professional life in 1977 and go to California in order to have an analysis with Wilfred Bion. So in his first session he said,

"I do not know quite why I am here, but I think you will be able to understand me and help me."

Bion replied,

"If you knew why, you would not be here; you would not have wasted time coming here. You came to see me precisely because you do not know why you have come."

Bion's reply to my friend seems entirely right to me. It is also for me a reply that is very moving, because Bion had understood the soul of my friend's suffering. Personal understanding of that deep kind stirs my soul. That understanding of a deep kind is born, I believe, of true compassion. You may retort that many people who arrive at the analyst's consulting-room *do* know why they have come. But do they? I think my friend was probably more self-aware than most of us. Not many of us arrive and say that we do not know why we have come for psychoanalysis. Most patients come with a particular complaint. One says that he is coming because relations with his wife are very bad. Another says that she comes because she wants to have a baby and believes that her difficulty in conceiving may be due to emotional reasons. Another comes saying he is devastated because his wife has just left him. Another comes because she is upset because, in a psychiatric assessment, she was diagnosed as being bi-polar. Another comes because he has suddenly become terrified of dying; another comes because he has been enormously depressed and friends have counselled her to approach a psychoanalyst. Yet, after a few weeks of conversation with the psychoanalyst, it becomes clear that these are just the "cover story". None of these people know why they are consulting the psychoanalyst. They produce a reason because it seems a bit absurd to tumble into the consulting-room and say,

"Oh, doctor, I am here, but I don't know why."

There is distress, but at the heart of it is a cloudy darkness. I do not know the wherefore of my distress.

So we reach this very odd conclusion: that the core of our distress lies in the fact that we do not know the reason for it. I think this is what we mean when we use that pale, passionless word "problem" to describe my situation when I decide to visit a psychoanalyst or a psychotherapist. So it begins to look as though the word "problem" may be right after all. I am suffering, yes, that's true, but . . . the reason for it is obscure, so there is something enigmatic about it, so we call it a problem. We will stick to that word as the best we have, but it does sound a bit intellectual—a bit as if it might be a mathematician speaking, and that with some cunning manipulation of a quadratic equation it could be solved. No, it is not a mere intellectual difficulty. Our emotions are in it here. Our emotions are in distress, and we know not why. We need to embrace the fact that it is a problem that troubles our spirit, that disturbs the heart. That is the meaning we give it when we call it a problem.

Now we move on to the next part of our quest. How is it that I am able to resolve this distress through speaking to another? There seems to be some inherent sense here that the act of communicating with another will help to alleviate the distress, which, according to what we have formulated, means that, in some mysterious way, this communication illuminates the darkness—that if the kernel of the distress lies in our ignorance of its cause, then there seems to be some intuition that talking to another may be able to replace night-time with daylight. How are we to understand this? Is it that the person we speak to will know what we do not know? or is it that the act of communication itself functions as an illuminator? I will take these two possibilities in turn.

The first hypothesis is that the person I speak to will know what I do not know. I think this is the hypothesis that most of us have tucked away inside us. I go to the dentist because I have a pain in one of my lower molars. I believe that he will know why I am having this pain. He looks at the tooth, takes an X-ray, and tells me that I have a large cavity with decay in it and that it will need a filling. So I am right: he does have knowledge that I do not have and is able through it to remedy the trouble. It is the same if I go to a doctor with stomach pains. If, on the other hand, I am in legal difficulties, then I go to a lawyer. He has knowledge that I do not have, and with his help I am able to solve my dilemma. Is it the case, though, that when I go to a psychoanalyst, he knows what I do not know? He knows the cause of my suffering? I think this needs some careful examination.

Now, as it happens, in my psychoanalytic role I do have some general theories as to why someone is suffering mentally. I believe that if, in childhood, some disaster has overtaken me, then I shall later suffer consequences of a mental kind; I have read my Bowlby, and even my Ainsworth, my Fonagy, and my Mary Target, so I believe that if someone has been severely neglected in babyhood, it will have a deleterious effect on the personality. I have read Frances Tustin, who believed that a premature rupture of the infant from its mother wounded the soul of the infant in a way that remained damaging for the rest of its life. I believe that if someone has sustained a loss of someone close to her, she will suffer. I believe that a serious accident will leave someone damaged. I believe that if someone is unable to love, he will suffer. These are general principles. They are abstract. They are truths that are up in the sky. They only acquire meaning when enfleshed in the details of a person's life experience. A doctor can probably say of most of his patients that they are suffering from an illness, but it is the particular illness that the doctor needs to know in order to offer an effective remedy to his patient. However, even if one of them seems to the psychoanalyst clearly correct in this one particular individual who has come for a consultation, yet . . . it is impossible that he would know the form that this may have taken. This is only possible through unravelling the story.

I am still proceeding on the basis of the first hypothesis. Let us say that the psychoanalyst diagnoses that the patient is suffering because her mother died giving birth to her; he knows that, and also that the patient thinks that this is the source of her difficulties. What is the medicine that the psychoanalyst prescribes? Well, I think we all know that the psychoanalyst does not prescribe a medicine. We also know that if he tells his patient that the source of her difficulties is that her mother died giving birth to her, that also remains a piece of dissociated knowledge that has no curative effect. Very early on Freud discovered that declaring to the patient the hidden cause of his distress was no good. He says that

> in the earliest days of analytic technique we took an intellectualist view of the situation. We set a high value on the patient's knowledge of what he had forgotten, and in this we made hardly any distinction between our knowledge of it and his. We thought it a special piece of good luck if we were able to obtain information about the forgotten childhood trauma from other sources—for instance, from parents or nurses or the seducer himself—as in some cases it was possible to do; and we hastened to convey the information and proofs of its correctness to the patient, in the certain expectation of thus bringing the neurosis and the treatment to a rapid end. It was a severe disappointment when the expected success was not forthcoming. How could it be that the patient, who now knew about his traumatic experience, nevertheless still behaved as if he knew

no more about it than before? . . . there was no choice but to cease attributing to the fact of knowing, in itself, the importance that had previously been given to it. [1913c, pp. 141–142]

So the idea that the problem is solved once the clinician has imparted knowledge to the patient seems to have a defect somewhere. We may all smile in a rather superior way and say that we sophisticated therapists all know that the clinician does not just dish out a piece of knowledge to the patient in the same way as a doctor hands out a prescription. Yet are we sure that we are free of this assumption? How many of us are attached to the theoretical position of a Bowlby, a Jung, a Melanie Klein, a Heinz Kohut, a Winnicott? I remember well and with some shame trying to force the medicine of Winnicott upon one of my patients until she finally managed to drill it into my thick head that this was no solution to her problem. I am struck by the fact that instead of trying to grasp the patient's problem as he or she presents it, many of us act as I did on that occasion, and it does not solve the problem. Freud said the reason was that the patient's consciousness has no connection to "the place where the repressed recollection is in some way or other contained" (1913c, p 142). I would like to emphasize his words *in some way or other contained*. I believe that the imagery that words conjure up in our minds are frequently responsible for directing us along the wrong path of thinking. The idea here is that the repressed experience exists in a similar form to that experience within consciousness: just the same, but just blocked off from our consciousness. Sometimes Freud spoke in this way, so the image is of an experience that is just the same as it is in consciousness but blocked off from consciousness by a barrier that was called *"repression"* when considered objectively and *"resistance"* when considered subjectively. However, it is clear from these words of his—*"in some way or other contained"*—that Freud was more open-minded about it. There is in those words some thought that the way in which it is contained in the unconscious may not be in the same mode as occurs in consciousness. But his central point here is that the patient's problem, the patient's neurosis, the patient's distress is not alleviated or resolved through imparting knowledge. I do not think this is absolute, and we shall have to come back to the idea. In the process there is most likely some imparting of knowledge, but this is not the central way in which the problem is resolved. Freud emphasized this point again in his paper on *The Unconscious:*

> If we communicate to a patient some idea which he has at one time repressed but which we have discovered in him, our telling him makes at first no change in his mental condition. Above all it does not remove the repression nor undo its effects [1915e, p. 175]

So where are we? That the core of the patient's problem is that we do not know the reason for the distress but we seem to have learned something else: that the imparting of knowledge does not resolve it. This would suggest that it is not the knowledge in itself but, rather, something about the process of acquiring knowledge that is crucial. Again Freud does indicate something about this:

> there is no lifting of the repression until the conscious idea, after the resistances have been overcome, has entered into connection with the unconscious memory-trace. It is only through the making conscious of the latter itself that success is achieved. [1915e, pp. 175–176]

This does seem to me very crucial. When sitting in the psychoanalyst's chair, I think I know something, yet if I impart this knowledge as I have it in my mind, it will do no good. Let us take an example. From the awe-struck way in which a patient speaks to me, I say to myself: she idealizes me, and I say this to her, but I find that it is just as ineffective as those pieces of knowledge that Freud gave up imparting to his patients a hundred years ago. We tend to smile patronizingly at Freud's naïveté, yet I have frequently found myself doing exactly the same thing, and I have heard many clinical presentations where I have heard the same naïveté expressed.

I think the implication is that the way that something exists in the unconscious is not the same as the way it exists in consciousness. In fact, I believe that we should put the matter the other way about: that it is because entities are in a particular form that they are not capable of being grasped in consciousness. We shall come to this in greater detail when we consider, in chapter 2, the difference between entities that are aggregates and those that are unified or coherent.

Let us move on, then, to the second hypothesis, which posits that the communication itself functions as an agent of illumination.

In a paper on symbolism Marion Milner says that if you take a pencil and put a mark upon a piece of paper, it begins to *speak back to you*. The very action, emanating from a desire inside, that ends in an external epiphany elaborates the act into something more fulsome and developed. It is like a small seed that remains dry and impenetrable while it lies upon a stone in the sun, but when it is thrust into damp soil it sprouts into a plant with beautiful blue flowers. All this magnificence was in the seed but invisible, impenetrable; but when it is planted into this favourable environment, the largeness and variety congealed within that small hard seed becomes accessible and visible to the senses. Astronomers tell us that thirteen million years ago there was a small, compact, extremely dense nugget of matter that exploded in the phenomenon that has been named the Big Bang. The huge variety of forms, of distances, of stars, of planets, and the whole vast universe exploded out of that unimaginably dense nugget. Something like this happens when I verbalize a thought or a feeling. As Charlotte Balkanyi (1964) says, verbalization that is the activity just prior to the act of speech is already the gathering of something indistinct into a recognizable form. This is the first movement in the act of communication, but it already suggests that in this initial act something amorphous is fashioned into a unified structure. I think we all know when there is something struggling in us to find a verbal form. The right word won't quite come. We try this word, that word, but we know that it is not right. The something that is striving to find its way out of the dark into the light has not found the key that will allow it to come into being. I verbalize as the first step in communication. In other words, communication puts a certain demand that I take the rough formless clay and mould it into a pattern. This very act of moulding it into a form enables it to cross over the space from you to me and puts me in possession of something that I did not have. I had it, yet did not have it. Freud (1914d, pp. 12–15) spoke about the way in which it is possible for someone to have a piece of knowledge within him and yet not know that he has it, and this has always struck me as very significant:

> There was some consolation for the bad reception accorded to my contention of a sexual aetiology in the neuroses . . . in the thought that I was taking up the fight for a new and original idea. But, one day, certain memories gathered in my

mind which disturbed this pleasing notion, but which gave me in exchange a valuable insight into the processes of human creative activity and the nature of human knowledge.

Freud goes on to explain that the original idea was not actually his: rather, it had been passed on to him over a period of years by three men whom he respected: by Josef Breuer, by Jean-Martin Charcot, and, finally, by Rudolf Chrobak, an eminent gynaecologist at Vienna University:

> These three men had all communicated to me a piece of knowl-edge which, strictly speaking, they themselves did not possess. Two of them later denied having done so when I reminded them of the fact; the third (the great Charcot) would probably have done the same if it had been granted me to see him again. But these three identical opinions, which I had heard without understanding, had laid dormant in my mind for years, until one day they awoke in the form of an apparently original dis-covery.

Freud then goes on to describe how, on three separate occasions, these three men had transmitted their ideas of the sexual aetiology of the neuroses—even though they had no conscious knowledge of this.

Breuer had told Freud that he was treating a woman who

> was behaving in such a peculiar way in society that she had been brought to him for treatment as a nervous case. He con-cluded: "These things are always *secrets d'alcove!*" I asked him in astonishment what he meant, and he answered by explain-ing the word *alcove* (marriage-bed) to me, for he failed to realize how extraordinary the *matter* of his statement seemed to me.

Freud then goes on to describe how, some years later, he overheard Charcot telling Paul Brouardel about

> a young married couple from a distant country in the East—the woman a severe sufferer, the man either impotent or exceeding-ly awkward. *"Tâchez donc,"* I heard Charcot repeating, *"je vous assure, vous y arriverez."* Brouardel . . . must have expressed his astonishment that symptoms like the wife's could have been produced by such circumstances. For Charcot suddenly broke out with great animation: *"Mais, dans des cas pareils c'est toujours la chose génitale, toujours . . . toujours . . . toujours"* . . .

Amazed, Freud said to himself:

"Well, but if he knows that, why does he never say so?"

A year later, having begun his medical career in Vienna, Freud was asked to treat one of Chrobak's patients, a woman with attacks of meaningless anxiety who could only function if she knew where her doctor was every minute of the day. Chrobak explained to Freud that

> the patient's anxiety was due to the fact that although she had been married for eighteen years she was still *virgo intacta*. The husband was absolutely impotent. . . . The sole prescription for such a malady, he added, is familiar enough to us, but we cannot order it. It runs: "*R. Penis normalis dosim repetatur!*"

Freud goes on to say that in recounting the above his purpose was not, of course, to saddle others with the responsibility for the concept of a sexual aetiology for neuroses:

> I am well aware that it is one thing to give utterance to an idea once or twice in the form of a passing *aperçu*, and quite another to mean it seriously—to take it literally and pursue it in the face of every contradictory detail, and to win it a place among accepted truths. It is the difference between a casual flirtation and a legal marriage with all its duties and difficulties. [Freud, 1914d, pp. 12–15]

It is worth asking why these three men—Breuer, Chrobak, and Charcot—did not understand what they knew? I believe it is that it did not fit in with their theory. Their theory blinded them to the significance of what they knew. This suggests that a piece of knowledge may not be understood and its significance allowed to startle the mind unless it is within a pattern of understanding to which it is related.

I think we need to try to understand this a bit better because what is being suggested here is that something is only understood if it is within a *"common denominator"* pattern—that a theory is an invisible bond that unites a series of discrete elements, but such a theory can be of two kinds:

1. one that claims to be the *common denominator* of the elements that it encompasses but is not;

2. a theory that claims to be the *common denominator* of the discrete
    elements and fulfils that claim and is the right instrument for
    the job that needs to be done.

Let us look at these in greater detail. Let us start with the purpose:
that is, the job to be done. In this case, let us say that the job that
Breuer, Chrobak, and Charcot were trying to accomplish was to relieve their patients of a neurosis. Speaking very basically, they had
a theory that neurosis was due to some anatomical difficulty, and
that this would be relieved through electrical treatment or hydro-
therapy. This was, at any rate, so with Breuer and Chrobak. Charcot believed that the patient could be cured of hysteria through
hypnotic suggestion. So we have two different theories here, but
each of them had a piece of knowledge that was idiosyncratic. It
was not part of any theoretical system; it was a piece of folklore
known to the man in the street but not to the man of science. It
reminds me of William Hazlitt's essay *The Ignorance of the Learned*,
where he says:

> You will hear more good things on the outside of a stage-coach
> from London to Oxford, than if you were to pass a twelve-
> month with the undergraduates, or heads of colleges, of that
> famous university; and more *home* truths are to be learnt from
> listening to a noisy debate in an ale-house, than from attending
> to a formal one in the House of Commons. [1908, p. 75]

A similar point has been made by the philosopher, Maurice
Blondel:

> whoever abuses the prestige of a magic world before simple
> folk and makes himself their guide, as if the scientist knew
> more about the secret of life than the least of the humble. No
> matter what we do, we shall never live only by scientific ideas.
> [1984, p. 92]

And it has been said, I think correctly, that one of Freud's contributions was to make common folklore medically acceptable, or at
least more acceptable than it was. So, in this case, the idiosyncratic
piece of knowledge was that neurosis, or certain neurotic symp-
toms, were caused by sexual frustration. This was something that
the man in the street knew; it was something that the-man-in-the-
street-within-the-scientist also knew; but it was something that

the scientist, dissociated from the man-in-the-street, did not know. The scientist and the man in the street were in watertight compartments. So, it would only be known, truly known, if the knowledge of the man-in-the-street was in communication with the scientist. If these two were in contact with each other, then the knowledge of the man-in-the-street would influence the scientist in such a way that the one would be a true representation of the other. The philosopher R. G. Collingwood defines science as "a body of systematic or orderly thinking about a determinate subject matter" (1969, p. 4). So science is the procedure whereby thinking is focused upon a defined object and organized in an orderly way. The object—in this case, the knowledge that sexual frustration causes neurosis—exercises its influence upon the thinking process in such a way that the thinking and the object of knowledge interact with one another. So we come back to our formulation at the beginning that

a piece of knowledge may not be understood and its significance allowed to startle the mind unless it is within a pattern of understanding to which it is related.

. . . that we come truly to know something only through its interrelation with other things or that the one known thing needs to be connected up with other functions within the mind.

These three scientists, then, have failed to take up a piece of common knowledge, reflect upon it, and elaborate it in such a way that it connects with other elements so that there is a resulting coherence. So two of those men, Breuer and Chrobak, had a theory that bodily turbulence or bodily relaxation would cure the neurosis: neurosis for them was the product of some bodily malfunction. Charcot believed that neurosis was brought about by suggestion, particularly hypnotic suggestion, and that it could be eliminated through such a procedure. He believed that neurosis was, therefore, psychologically determined. However, he knew, as did the other two men, that the cause of the neurosis lay in sexual frustration, but with all three of them it lay there as a piece of anecdotal knowledge. The man-in-the-street within them had no intercourse with the scientist within them.

We started this talk by saying that someone approaches a clinician because she has a problem. An understanding of *her* problem is the foundation stone for its resolution. The clinician needs an instrument within himself through which he is able to understand her problem. The nature of this instrument is therefore crucial. In the case of Breuer and Chrobak, they were applying a remedy that had no relation to their patients' problem, yet they had within them some idea of the problem and its solution, but something was preventing them from reaching the solution that lay inside them. That which was most in them, most at hand, was being discarded in favour of a remedy that, truly speaking, they did not believe would restore health to the patient. What we are saying here is that the *received remedy* gets in the way of these men applying the remedy that lies within them. The *common denominator* is not a common denominator at all, because it does not refer to the problem. Before coming to how we find the true *common denominator*, I want to show, if I can, that the false path that Breuer, Chrobak, and Charcot were all following is just as present today as it was then: that many of us clinicians are failing because we are applying a received remedy that has no relevance to our patient's problem. I will give some examples of this.

In 2002 an article appeared in the *International Journal of Psycho-Analysis* entitled "The thread of Depression through the Life and Works of Leo Tolstoy" by Annie Anargyros-Klinger. I wrote a letter, which was published in a subsequent issue (Symington, 2002a). In my letter I take up several points, but the one I wish to focus on here is her view that Tolstoy's depression arose from the fact that his mother had died when he was 18 months old and that he

> may have remained fixated at a primitive oral stage with its succession of cannibalistic fantasies that were extremely alarming in terms of their destructive taking over of the object. The presence in him of the dead object, faecalised, formed a psychic pole of attraction and fascination due to the libidinal stimulation linked to the original trauma. [Anargyros-Klinger, 2002]

There is a series of theories here: that it is a trauma for a baby to lose his mother at the age of 18 months; that he remained fixated at that infantile stage of development; that there are cannibalistic fantasies operating at this stage; that the dead mother has remained psychically present within his personality; that this dead mother has become "faecalized"; and, lastly, that this original trauma had set up a libidinal stimulation that held him prisoner within it. The complaint I made in my letter of reply was that Tolstoy himself had a theory as to why he was depressed, and that the analyst had not listened to his own understanding of it.

This is just one example of where a theory is imposed to explain the problem, but it is not the person's own problem. It is a solution that is imposed from without but does not come as an answer to this individual person's dilemma. There are many theories of this nature that are imposed in this way. I will look at just a few of them. One of Kohut's ideas, for instance, is that a patient's under-valuation of himself is frequently due to a lack of mirroring from the mother during his infancy. One of Melanie Klein's ideas is that the infant is in terror of the presence of the death instinct within him, which threatens to annihilate him, and that this is the origin of panic. Winnicott has the idea that psychosis is an environmental deficiency disease. Bion had the idea that the psychotic patient had an overdose within him of the death instinct. Any of these ideas may be true; they may apply in certain circumstances, but they are not abstract enough to act as instruments that will lead to an understanding of the patient's problem. What I mean is that if I try to apply one of these to this patient, then I shall, almost certainly, be forcing the patient into the mould of the particular model I am trying to apply. In the case I instanced of the article about Tolstoy, the analyst was forcing Tolstoy into a mould made up of a series of Freud's theories.

Freud and Bion both recommended a particular state of mind that the clinician needs to be in. Freud referred to it as *free-floating attention*, Bion as *reverie*. There is a state of *inquiry* governing the state. The *inquiry* is a state where the mind is searching for a model that fits the particular problem, so there is an idea here that it is understandable. There is a principle: that an act of understanding is possible if the right imaging category can be found. The act of understanding occurs when the image is close enough to enable that leap which constitutes the act. The principle here is that the act of understanding results from imagery that is close to the problem-atic area but is itself a leap from it. There is in this moment of leap a construction of a new mental reality. So the abstract principle is that the mind is able to construct a mental reality from imagery that bears the form-lines enabling construction.

But the way I have put this may give the wrong impression. What I mean is that it may give the impression that I am, in a detached way, concerned with this person, this person sitting opposite me, that I am concerned with her problem—not with a problem that in any way concerns me. After all, I am a psychoanalyst, I have been analysed, so I no longer have any problems. Of one thing I am certain: that no problem will ever be solved if that is my stance. If I have given the impression that by *inquiry* I mean something like that, then I must immediately correct it and I shall attempt it by an example. I shall start with a story I was once told that chills the blood.

> A man and his wife lived in a large house at the end of a long winding gravel drive. The wife was driving home one day, and as she came up the drive, she came upon a huge boulder that her car was unable to pass; so she got out of the car and walked up to the house and told her husband. However, as soon as he heard her stopping her car, two accomplices rolled the boulder away and hid it behind some bushes. She told her husband that there was a huge boulder in the drive, so he said he would come and investigate with her. When they arrived at the car, there was no boulder, and he said to her that she must have been hallucinating. The husband had done this, along with other such pranks, because he was determined to drive his wife mad.

If I see something and someone tells me that I am wrong, that the thing is not there, or if I feel something but someone tells me that I am feeling something else, it is capable of driving me mad. It is one of the reasons why I am careful never to tell a patient that she is feeling guilty or denying her feelings of sadness, especially when she replies

"But I am not feeling guilty . . ."

or:

"I don't think I am sad or pushing away any feelings that I am . . ."

If I do that, I am acting like the malevolent husband, though in a more subtle way. The point is this, though: that if I am told some-thing that is against what I perceive, think, or feel and am told that my own perception, thought, or feeling is wrong, it is capable of driving me mad. Now, this is something I knew, but I was puzzled as to quite why it should drive someone mad. I knew it as a fact but did not quite know the reason, but I wondered why it was, and this had been something I had wondered about for some years. I did not get up every morning and rush to psychiatric textbooks looking anxiously for an answer, but it was something I *wondered* about. This *wondering* is a state similar to that described by Freud as *free-floating attention* and by Bion as *reverie*. This *wondering* is about certain features of human life that are at once private and personal and also interpersonal and inherent in all cultures and historical periods.

Then one day I was treating a woman whose mother fell preg-nant with her subsequent to a one-night stand. Her mother was a Catholic and therefore would not have an abortion. From her earliest years my patient's mother used frequently to say she loved her, but there were numerous things that contradicted this. She was a latchkey child: she would come home from school and have to let herself into the house and make her own tea; her mother would promise her a special present for Christmas but would get drunk the previous evening, and in the morning there were no presents. . . . The patient in her adolescence went on drugs, contracted syphilis through promiscuous sex, and made suicide attempts. One day she said to me:

> "You know, it would have been much better for me if my mother had told me that she had not wanted me. I could have dealt with that."

When she said that, I believed I had the beginning of an answer to my enquiry. I understood that the mother's statements that she loved her so clearly contradicting her conduct towards her daughter had been a powerful determinant in my patient's "mad-ness"—her drug addiction, promiscuity, and suicide attempts. But I understood further that if her mother had told her the truth, it would have been preferable. I think there were two intersecting reasons for this, which lead me to a series of important principles. The first is that if her mother had told her that she had not wanted her, she would have trusted her; she would have trusted because what her mother was then saying made sense of the behaviour that she had experienced from her mother; that love of another is only possible when the words spoken fit with the emotional behaviour. And, lastly, that it drives someone mad if she is not able to love.

This principle was enunciated by George Eliot in her novel *Middlemarch*. The love of Lydgate for Rosamund is a sub-plot of the novel. Rosamund is a *femme fatale,* and after a time Lydgate realizes that she does not love him but far worse, says George Eliot, is: "the certainty 'she will never love me much', is easier to bear than the fear 'I shall love her no more'" (Eliot, 1973, p. 702).

The overarching principle here is that it drives not only her, this patient of mine, mad, but that anyone goes into madness if they are not able to love. This answer to my questioning came through an understanding of this woman's problem, but my state of enquiry related not just to this woman sitting in front of me but to something general that applied to her, to me, and to people across cultures and back down through history for at least eleven millennia, or since the dawning of civilization. So the principle that madness arises if someone is not able to love has sufficient abstraction within it to apply to a description of humanity in all its many forms. It is capable of being a common denominator that entirely respects the individuality and freedom of each person and as a principle is capable of being used to solve each individual patient's problem and does not force any individual into a framework that does not fit.

There is a further principle that is closely linked to this: that as soon as someone starts to love, she experiences mental pain. It may be sadness, it may be guilt, it may be regret, it may be disappointment, or it may be shame. Hatred expels the pain, whereas love embraces it. Therefore one reason why love is avoided is because it opens the person to pain. Madness, then, is an anaesthetic against pain. These, then, are interrelated principles.

There is another ancillary principle that is implied in what my patient said about her mother. It was clear that something prevented her mother from embracing the truth that she had not wanted this child of hers. It may have been that this is not a feeling that a mother is supposed to have, and here is another ancillary principle: that under constraint a truth cannot be embraced. For it to be capable of being embraced, someone needs to be entirely free of constraint. And then a further principle arises from this: that had her mother been able to embrace it and thus to say it to her child, her hatred would then have been contained within her own psyche and not discharged; her child's experience would, then, have been quite different. Instead of experiencing neglectful or hateful activities of the mother, she would have known a distress of her mother's. Mother's distress would not have been expressed in neglectful acts towards her daughter but transformed into inner knowledge. So the principle here is that the encompassing of a truth within the psyche generates understanding towards the other. So my patient's experience as a child would have been different.

Another ancillary principle flows from this: that I see the world through the lens of my own psychological structure. If that structure is based on hate and discharge, the way I see the world is quite different from the way I see the world if I have embraced what is within me.

These, then, are the abstract principles that I am able to use as instruments to solve the problem that my patient brings me. As they apply to me as much as to my patient, they give me a platform from which to judge the state of self-awareness. Knowing myself, to the extent to which I am able to achieve it, is the fundamental yardstick through which I am able to understand the problems of my patients.

If the analyst's or psychotherapist's psychological place is in the sphere of these principles, then from this viewpoint—which is either deeper or higher than psychological models proper—all of them can be encompassed. At the moment within psychoanalytic discourse the models are restricted within a narrow field. We are all familiar with Freud's theory of repression, with Jung's typology, with Kohut's theory of mirroring, with Melanie Klein's theory of the paranoid-schizoid position and the depressive position, with Bion's theory of container–contained, but these are just those models contained within the official psychoanalytic "textbooks"; there are many other models that are often apt. For instance, classical learning theory is often applicable, as is Piaget's theory of object constancy, Arnold Zweig's theory of intensified passion in the handicapped individual, Blondel's theory that emotional action takes its colouring from the object towards which it tends, Macmurray's theory that the self is an agent that produces thought, Tolstoy's theory that suicide is the outcome of extreme narcissism, Hermann Hesse's view that suicide is a state of mind rather than a particular act, the Buddha's theory of *dukka*, the historian Arthur Bryant's view that stifled creativity leads to destructiveness. The higher-order principles that I have tried to enunciate enable the clinician to encompass all these and many other different models. I have entitled this "An Intellectual Solution", and these higher principles require the intellectual capacity to abstract and yet, paradoxically, grasping one of these principles is only possible through a personal act of comprehension. It is not something I can ever attain through rote learning or through mere ingestion. Although highly abstract and intellectual, yet its core is emotional and personal. It is abstract but not only intellectual but also emotional. The relational nature of emotions comes in chapter 2.

I often hear someone saying, "I work with an object relations model" or "I use a self psychology model" or "I work with a Jungian framework"—and this will nearly always mean that the patient is being tailored to fit the model rather than an attitude or perspective that will be syntonic to the patient. This is because all of these models lack the abstractness and emotional depth necessary to serve as instruments capable of encompassing and illuminating the subjectivity of the other. Now, it may sound as though these abstract principles are intellectual and not emotional, but this is incorrect: as they are grasped and can only be grasped personally, they are in their very essence emotional. The capacity, then, to grasp these higher principles become the guarantee against fitting the patient to the clothes rather than the clothes to the patient.

I want, however, to enter a caution concerning what I have said about "higher principles" of organization. It is that there are two ways in which these higher principles can be misused. The "higher principle" may be embraced in a sentimental way or in a way that fails to apply it in rigorous detail to the factual circumstance of a person's life. "All we need is love", someone cries in a fashion that denies that there is hatred, violence, and enmity in the world. The other misuse is to use the higher principle in a concrete way as a sensuous model. So, in this case, the word "love" is applied in an erotic sense rather than in an overarching sense, as is applied in the word *agape*. I have elsewhere called this as the error of the misplaced absolute, and I have seen it referred to as making that which is secondary into what is primary. The mediaeval mystic and scholar Meister Eckhart referred to this as "the root of all fallacy" (Kelley, 1977, p. 42). So, for instance, one might describe as primary the psychoanalyst's emotional receptivity to the other, whereas the custom that a session should last 50 minutes or that a patient should lie on a couch are secondary.

We started by saying that inherent in a problem was something that was unknown. We have taken up one aspect of this: those occasions when there is an idiosyncratic piece of knowledge that is known yet not known because it does not interpenetrate with other pieces of knowledge and joined together and held by a high theoretical principle with which it and the other parts are consonant. One level, then, at which a problem can be solved is when a piece of knowledge is grafted into its correct position within a theoretical principle of understanding. When this occurs—when a discrete piece of knowledge is suddenly seen fitting into a wider unified pattern—the mind is illuminated with a healing light. The common denominator illuminates the discrete element, and the latter gives life and energy to the underlying theory. There is a moment of love and excitement. I end by quoting a passage from the novel *Beware of Pity* by Stefan Zweig:

> I felt as one does when the curtains in a dark room are suddenly drawn aside, and the sunlight is so blinding that everything swims purple before one's eyes and one reels in the dazzling glare of the almost inconceivable flood of light. [1939/1953, p. 161]

However, I think this is only a partial explanation. It is does not give attention to the interpersonal. It does not highlight the communicative aspect of emotional life or bring into focus the significance of talking to another person. We have to bring into connection the higher principles together with the person to person encounter. We must leave that to the next and subsequent chapters.

CHAPTER TWO

The meaning of emotion

The question: *How is it that someone who has a problem is able to resolve it through conversation with another?*

"as always happens in the world, what was at first a happy accident or means of survival, is promptly transformed and used as an instrument of progress . . ."

Pierre Teilhard de Chardin [1960, p. 104]

We have formulated that at the heart of someone's dilemma is the fact that she does not know the reason for her suffering and that this is the prime motive that decides her to communicate with a fellow human being. We further determined that we only truly know something if it is in relation to elements that are consonant with it through a *common denominator*—a higher-order emotional principle that links them all into a meaningful whole. We concluded that the unknown could become known through being thus connected to other constituents of a unified pattern: that which was alien and therefore senseless had now achieved "brotherhood" and become meaningful. The dispelling of ignorance has been quite central to Eastern philosophy, and I think has been a key goal in Buddhism and Hinduism and also of the Scholastic Philosophers of the Middle Ages, such as Thomas Aquinas and Albert the Great. It follows from what we said earlier that what is senseless is in part a function of its being isolated from other elements that we know—that if something is alien in the personality, it will not be grasped; also if it is a stranger to the norms of the culture, it will not be comprehended. This was understood in a very profound way by the author of the *Zohar*. The *Zohar* is a Jewish Kabbalist text thought to have been written by Moses de León in fourteenth-century Spain. He says moral evil is "always either something which becomes separated and isolated, or something which enters into a relation for which it is not made" (Scholem, 1995, p. 236). This for me is a very profound understanding and one that is in harmony with psychoanalytic thinking about those parts of the self that are "split off", but it adds another dimension. It is that the injurious element in the personality is so *because it is alienated*—in other words, it is not evil or, in our more familiar language, destructive inherently, but because it remains distanced from other parts of the personality. This would mean that when we talk about a greedy part or an envious part, we are at the same time saying that the underpinning of these vicious aspects is that they are alienated elements, and therefore the prime task is not to banish them but, rather, to embrace them, and that the very act of linking them together changes their character—so, for instance, greed would become courage and envy would become respect. Those familiar with Bion will realize that this is very much in line with what he says about attacks on linking. One has to ask why someone would want to keep something alienated to make what Bion says harmonize with what the author of the *Zohar* has said.

Moses de León had a profound insight in this regard. I want here to put in an aside. There is a tendency for us to think that all psychological insight sprang from Freud and his followers. I think Aldous Huxley was right when he said,

> One of the most extraordinary, because most gratuitous, pieces of twentieth-century vanity is the assumption that nobody knew anything about psychology before the days of Freud. But the real truth is that most modern psychologists understand

human beings less well than did the ablest of their predeces-
sors. [1980, p. 132]

So I want to endorse and give emphasis to this profound insight
hidden away in a text of the *Zohar*. I think his insight is correct
and of mind-blowing significance and will go a long way towards
answering our basic question, though it does not go into why
conversation with another is enabling. Clearly, in what I have just
said is the implication that alienation is in itself a source of suffering. But does the alienation not have some dimension other than
what is generally called "intellectual" or what I have referred to as
"higher-order emotional"? We did say that the placing of a piece
of knowledge within a meaningful pattern had in it an emotional
component, but the role of the other in the dialogue had scant
attention.

* * *

Now, I do not think we can get any further unless we examine
what we mean by something that we describe as *emotional*. It is
the things that we refer to most, that we speak about in our daily
conversation dozens of times, that often require the greatest mental
effort to define. So, ask someone, "What is a book?" or "What is
an aeroplane?" and he can tell you reasonably easily, but ask him
"What is Time?" or "What is Place?" and he will have to stretch
his mental powers to their very limits to attempt an answer. Phenomena like time or place are so much the fabric of our daily lives
into which we are inserted that we have the greatest difficulty in
extracting ourselves from ourselves so that we can see the contours
of what is most commonplace. Yet, if education is precisely that
very stretching of the mind that this involves, then, I believe, we
need to make the attempt. C. S. Lewis says this in the words of the
Senior Devil, Screwtape: "Aggravate that most useful human characteristic, the horror and neglect of the obvious" (1987, p. 20).

Such, I believe, is the case with the word *emotion*. So this chapter
is entirely devoted to the subject of emotion, and I think that if we
can reach the end with even a vague sketch of a definition, then we
shall be well equipped—or at least better equipped—to take a few
more strides along our pathway, the destination of which is to find
out why a problem can be solved through converse with another.

Someone rushes in and says,

"John Smith has just died of a heart attack."
Mary Twigley stands, listens, and asks quite coolly,
"When did it happen? and where?"
Joseph Rindbergh gasps and says,

"Oh how dreadful . . ."
then he lets out a scream and bursts into tears. A bystander listens and then goes and reports the event to his friend, Joanna Partridge, and after telling of John Smith's death, he says,

"When she heard, Mary Twigley was completely unemotional, but Joseph Rindbergh was very emotional. He let out a scream and burst into tears."

So Mary is described as *unemotional* and Joseph as *emotional*. What we seem to mean here is that Joseph is affected by the event, he is engaged in it, he is in relation to it. We suspect that he was a friend of John Smith, that he had a relationship with him, and now here it has been suddenly terminated, whereas Mary Twigley displayed no evidence of being affected by John Smith's death. So by *emotional* we seem to mean a connectedness, some bond engaging one person with another. But surely—I hear you say—it is language that connects one person with another. For instance, in the little vignette when someone rushes in and says that John Smith has just died of a heart attack, there has been a communication, but the effect of it upon Joseph Rindbergh is quite different from that upon Mary Twigley. What we are talking of, then, when we use the word *emotional* is a connection between one person and another, of which language is merely a representation—that this connection, which we call *emotional,* is invisible. It is a something that links one person to another and also something that is extremely powerful. If we went up into a church steeple and looked down upon the people milling around in the village square, we would see a cluster of isolated individuals: that which links one to the other is not visible to the eye; there is bond between individuals that cannot be seen.

We all know that the baby has a bond with its mother straight after birth and also before birth. The infant does not develop language for 12 to 18 months, but there is a bond there, a channel of communication between mother and baby. I think, then, that the *emotions* **are** that channel of communication. Different emotions are registers of the differing colours of that communication. Love, hate, anger, joy, peace, frustration, envy, contentment are the differing hues of that shared disclosure or, to use a musical analogy, different tones, different scales, of that intimate kinsmanship. So *emotion is* the communication between one person and another. Wilfred Bion asserts this point when he says, "An emotional experience cannot be conceived of in isolation from a relationship" (1962/1984, p. 42).

Each *emotion* can be thought of as a unit of that communication. The philosopher John Macmurray has emphasized the prelinguistic level of communication thus:

> It has commonly been asserted that what distinguishes us from the animals is the gift of speech. There is an obvious truth in this, but it has two defects if used for purposes of definition. The power of speech is sometimes defined as the capacity to express ourselves. This misses an essential point; for the power of speech is as much the capacity to understand what is said to us as it is to say things to other people. The ability to speak is then, in the proper sense, the capacity to enter into reciprocal communication with others. It is our ability to share our experience with one another and so to constitute and participate in a common experience. Secondly, speech is a particular skill; and like all skills it presupposes an end to which it is a means. No one considers that deaf-mutes lack the characteristic which distinguishes them as human beings from the animals. They are merely obliged to discover other means of communication than speech. Long before the child learns to speak he is able to communicate, meaningfully and intentionally, with his mother. In learning language, he is acquiring a more effective and more elaborate means of doing something which he already can do in a crude and more primitive fashion. If this were not so, not merely the child's acquiring of speech, but the very existence of language would be an inexplicable mystery. [1991, p. 60]

He almost reaches the point I am making. I take it a step further and say that when he refers to a *more elaborate means of doing something that he can already do in a crude and more primitive fashion,* I am saying that this *something* is what we know as the emotions.

One can think of human beings under two aspects: the instinct for survival and the linkage that exists between human beings. The latter, the linkage, is the sphere of the *emotional.* Of course there is an intercourse between the two: the survival of the individual is bound up with the community of which he is a part. His own survival will be linked to that of others, but there is an important matter here. Is my communication with another for the purpose of survival alone? or does it have another purpose? Is it an end in itself? I want to argue here that it is—or, more correctly, that it has been taken up for—an end in itself.

You will notice here that I am defining an emotion as an invisible or non-sensuous channel of communication. This is a different way of defining emotion from that which comes to us from William James and, more recently, Antonio Damasio, who defines emotion as "a collection of changes in body state connected to particular mental images that have activated a specific brain system" (1994, p. 145), which is essentially different from the way I am defining it. In his definition, Damasio is in company with Freud, William James, Donald Hebb, J. B. Watson, and nearly all psychiatrists, psychologists, and psychoanalysts. The quote I have given you from Macmurray is different. He holds that there is a communication between human beings that is based upon a different channel of knowledge from the way any of us processes information about the nonhuman world. Even that is not quite correct, but we shall leave it like that for a moment. The view held by Freud, by William James, by J. B. Watson, and by nearly all classical psychology and contemporary philosophy is that we process information from other human beings in exactly the same way as we process information about the inanimate world around us or the nonhuman animate world. We take in information through our senses and synthesize this into a unitary pattern (I elaborate this more fully in chapter 5), and we do this in exactly the same way whether the external stimulus is a sunset, a cockatoo squawking, a train passing through a tunnel, or another human being I am conversing with. Chapter 1 could have been put into that context without disturbing anything that I said in it, but what is being brought in here is another dimension. Although the majority of philosophers, psychologists, and nearly all psychiatrists espouse the view that stimuli from the human as well as the nonhuman environment are processed similarly, there have been a few figures—such as Max Weber, Wilhelm Dilthey, Maurice Blondel, and, in more recent times, such people as John Macmurray and Martin Buber—who believe that there is a special channel of communication existing between human beings. I think the first person to claim this was the Italian jurist and philologist Giambattista Vico, who held the Chair of Jurisprudence in Naples in the early years of the eighteenth century. Vico held that there are two distinct and independent methods of inquiry. Through one we penetrate into the products of human creation and into the person-hood of another, and he called this method of inquiry *"scienza"* or "knowledge *per causas"*. We enter the world of the other, which becomes floodlit with new knowledge. The other form of knowledge is what he called *"coscienza"*, which is knowledge of the external world acquired by the observer from outside.

At that time thinkers were under the sway of Descartes, who said that we know the natural world best because we process it through our senses, but Vico, a lone voice, challenged this and said: "Look, we can understand much better—because from the inside—those things that human beings have made." That which is outside human invention is always outer, but those things that man has invented and created can be understood inwardly. The creator understands what he has created much better than a piece of nature unfashioned by mankind.

* * *

Roger Hausheer says of the first of these forms of inquiry that

> It is sui generis and can be described and analysed only in terms of itself. It cannot be yielded by nor translated into Cartesian or a Newtonian or any similar system which correlates things and events from "outside" in terms of causal regularities. [1979, p. xxxi]

In a similar way, Isaiah Berlin says Vico formulated the matter thus:

> we communicate with others because we can and do grasp in some direct fashion, less or more successfully, the purpose and meaning of their words, their gestures, their signs and symbols; for if there were no communication, there would be no language, no society, no humanity. [Berlin, 1979, p. 96]

Isaiah Berlin also says:

> He [Vico] uncovered a sense of knowing which is basic to all human studies; the sense in which I know what it is to be poor,

to fight for a cause, to belong to a nation, to join or abandon a church or a party, to feel nostalgia, terror, the omnipresence of a god, to understand a gesture, a work of art, a joke, a man's character. [p. 116]

Then Berlin makes this extremely important point:

Vico's ultimate claim to immortality: the principle according to which man can understand himself because, and in the process, of understanding his past—because he is able to reconstruct imaginatively . . . what he did and what he suffered, his hopes, wishes, fears, efforts, his acts and his works, both his own and of his fellows. [p. 114]

The viewpoint that holds that there is some special channel of communication between humans but not between a human and any nonhuman object seems to have had striking confirmation recently in an amazing study showing that people who were visually blind—a blindness caused by lesions of the occipital or parietal lobe—were nevertheless able to detect the difference between an angry face and a happy face (Damasio, 2003, p. 61, here quoting two studies by Vuilleumier & Schwartz, 2001a & 2001b; see also de Gelder, Vroomen, Pourtois, & Weiskrantz, 1999). Damasio says that in such cases the presence of the happy face or the angry face *breaks through* the barrier of blindness.

So human beings understand, and almost see, through imaginative reconstruction.

* * *

When I am listening to a patient, it is through imaginative *reconstruction* that I am able to understand. The interaction between us is one where a reconstruction is occurring. It is not a case of finding a fact that was already there, but one of reconstructing—making a new reality out of—the elements that are already there. So the act of understanding is not a realization of what was already there but, rather, the apprehension of a newly created reality. Consciousness is the product of this newly created reality. Self-knowledge also arises through this new creation in the way that a painter grasps and understands the landscape in front of him through the act of creating his painting, but that between two human beings is at the same time a creative act that gives a direct knowledge of the other.

This way of defining emotion is different from the usual way in which it is defined. The emotion is usually conceptualized as a body state. I conceptualize it as an action that in itself cannot be seen, heard, smelt, tasted, or touched but is accompanied by bodily changes. This is the view of it taken by those who have developed a theory of action, and it is the view of it taken by Wilfred Bion. Some quotes from Bion support this point:

> The realities with which psycho-analysis deals, for example fear, panic, love, anxiety, passion, have no sensuous background, though there is a sensuous background (respiratory rate, pain, touch, etc.) that is often identified with them and then treated, supposedly scientifically. [1970, p. 89]

You will see that he says here that what he calls the "sensuous background" is often identified with the states of fear, love, panic, and anxiety, but he infers that this is a mistaken identification and, further, that this mistaken identification is then treated as if it were a scientific fact; but he advisedly uses the word *supposedly*—in other words, it is not scientific but, instead, a pseudo-science.

I want to go more deeply into this matter and start first by re-stating that the emotions are the connecting link between people. They *are* that connection. Having stated that, I want to argue with some force for the view that the emotions themselves are, as Bion states, non-sensuous entities: these channels of communication we call the emotions *are* the relationship. A relationship implies that there are two separate things and a space between them. At the neurological level, which we consider more closely in chapter 5, there is a *synapse*—a space—between two neurons. The space is what it says it is. There is nothing between the two things, and yet they are in relation to each other—so the relationship *is* the space or it is *in* the space. The space becomes something when it is between two entities, and yet it remains a space. The two entities are in relation to each other in and through the space, and yet, therefore, the space itself has no sensuous qualities—it is empty of sensuous quality. Bion takes this view when he says, "there are no sense-data directly related to psychic quality" (1962, p. 53).

* * *

The emotions are the foundation stone of the mind. Mind-stuff—or mind-vacuum might be better—is the relation between . . . well, we are thinking of human beings, but how did mind-stuff come to be? There are three views on this. One is that there is no such thing as mind in human beings but just brain: this theory is known as *physicalism* or *materialism*. Another view is that humans do have mind, but it came into existence at some animal stage. It exists in humans, in chimpanzees, in mammals, and down the family tree until . . . ? Those holding this view take mind down (rather pejorative?) to the birds. For some reason they do not take it as far as fish. In some magical way mind appeared with birds and presumably reptiles. This theory is known as *emergentism*. It suggests that mind emerged concurrently with the appearance of a central nervous system, but the sense I get is that the proponents of this view are stuck when it comes to explaining how mind started or first emerged. Somehow it appeared—perhaps created by God or some magical process. Then there is yet another view, which is the one I strongly favour. This theory has been called *panexperientialism*, and it has two core ideas: that mind and brain are just two ways of looking at one thing, and that mind-stuff exists in the most elemental particles of matter. Mind-stuff is the relation between things, and, granted this, then it is built into the very fabric of the universe. Charles Birch, who is Professor Emeritus of Biology from Sydney University, says this in his excellent little book called *Feelings*:

> There is no reason why we should not say than an electron is attracted to a proton. We mean that the electron takes into account internally the proton in its environment. The proposition is that all entities such as electrons, cells and humans have internal relations. They can all be called organisms. [1995, p. 79]

In this book he also shows that the composition of a carbon atom in a diamond is the same as the carbon atom in an enzyme, and yet the two have different properties. Birch says,

> The carbon atom in a diamond has relations to a multitude of carbon atoms around it. The carbon atom in an enzyme has relations to many different sorts of atoms in its environment. In each case the carbon atom is conceived to take into account internally those relations. [1995, pp. 77–78]

So the striking idea here is that the relationship to the surrounding objects enters into the internal being of the subject or original object.

He goes on to say that an aggregate is not internally influenced in this way, whereas an individual or a compound is. If we flow this upwards through to humans and take the idea that there are these two ways in which the human being can be composed—either on the aggregate model or the unified one—and, further, that the presence to me of the unified human being brings about a change in my internal structure whereas the presence of an *aggregate individual* does not, then we would be saying that there is something in the way humans are structured that is consistent with the forms of existence from subatomic particles to life on earth and through to the solar system. I feel strongly that this principle is elemental to understanding internal change within human beings; I argued for it in less scientific manner in two articles that appeared in the *Australasian Journal of Psychotherapy* (Symington, 2003a, 2003b). This alters in a radical way the notion of what it is that produces change in psychotherapy. The received tradition states that it is interpretation, but what is being said here is that the internal changes depend on whether the state of mind of the therapist or psychoanalyst is in aggregate mode or unified mode. This may also go some way to explaining why it is that the individual behaves differently depending on the group of which he is a member.

So the point is that emotions are the relations between human beings. The physical states that we often call emotions are accompaniments, but not the emotion itself. I come to this again in chapter 5, where I contrast this view with the dominant one that is held by William James and also by Damasio. I do not want to be diverted by this now, however, but continue to build up our argument and then reflect upon it. So—emotions are the connecting link between people, and the emotions are the foundation stone of the mind, which implies that mind is substantially a relation and one that has no sensuous qualities. This has been forcefully argued by the Canadian philosopher Peter March in his (privately circulated) paper *Mind as Relation*, who states it thus:

> If the mind were a system of physical relations between material objects, then, in a sense, the mind would not be visible. Consider first the very simple relation *in front of*. As let's take the example where someone says that one of her hands is in front of the other. It is true, in a sense, that this relation between

two objects is not itself visible—in the sense in which the objects themselves are visible. The relation exists, of course, but if we were asked to give the colour or the shape of the relation we would be stumped.

So, granting that we do say that we can *see* that someone is in front of another person and granting further that most physical relations are discovered using visual information, still, since they have neither colour nor shape, they violate our intuition, which suggests that everything which can be seen in the *primary sense* must have colour and shape.

In another sense these relations are invisible because the relevant relata are not easily observable. One can say that it is a visible fact that one hand can be seen to be in front of the other. But the relations of mind exists as relations between neural structures of the person and objects which are not part of the person's body, hence, and since these relata are not visible to the naked eye, the relations themselves are not visible. We can not see that one hand is in front of another if we can't see one of the hands.

What this means is that if the mind is a system of relations then we would be unable to give its colour or its shape, nor would we be able to detect the relevant relations by sight.

For me it is a very exciting idea that the emotions as the basis of mind are part of the stuff of the universe and that some correlate of this exists not only in all living organisms, but also right down into the internal constitution of atoms. I cannot myself imagine a more stimulating piece of research than a team made up of physicists, chemists, biologists, philosophers, and psychoanalysts whose aim would be deepen our understanding of this basic mind-stuff that permeates the structure of the universe, from the atom to the human being, with each discipline bringing forth information from its own object of enquiry.

* * *

Something extremely important happened in human development about 30,000 years ago. You may say that I need not go back as far as this: that this can no longer have an influence. If you hold that view, then you must also obliterate all talk of instincts, which go back much further—to our animal past, to the time before *hominization*. Human beings started to fashion their survival needs into a structured pattern, so that there was time and energy left over for . . . for what? Just let me give you the picture first. Probably starting in the Middle East, human groupings started to domesticate animals and to grow their own crops about 11,000 years ago, or 9,000 years before our present era (it being no longer politically correct to speak of BC). Instead of being hunter-gatherers, humans began to husband their food supply, so that it came within their own ownership. When this was achieved, not all their energy was devoted to their survival needs. One of the instruments that made civilization possible was leisure; it was also one of the first fruits of civilization.

What did *civilization* mean? It was that elements present in the human constitution for the purposes of survival began to be used *not* for survival, but *as ends in themselves.* Elements that had been a means became ends. It is easy to think how this is so of something like food. We eat food for our survival, and, in an extreme state of hunger, I might even eat baked beans and Marmite: it is food, after all. But once hunger is abated, I then decide to eat lobster and mayonnaise. In the second case I am not eating for the purpose of staving off hunger; survival is no longer the issue; I am eating for the pleasure of eating. The same can be said of sex. I have in my time even come across people who have had sex for its own pleasure and not to procreate. But the most important element that is subject to this process of being scooped up for its own sake is communication itself. Communication between one individual and another was for survival, to give alarm calls, to signal the presence of an animal that could be killed for the pot, and so on; but with the advent of civilization, communication, in its many different forms, became an end in itself. What may have originally been a yodelling call to signal danger in the mountains became the beginning of music, and a sign on a tree that there was a savage bear in the district then became the beginning of art. But if one thinks of music and art as different forms of communication, then communication becomes an end in itself. And if *emotion* is the basic unit of communication of which speech, music, and art are the representation, then *emotion* itself becomes an end in itself. Survival is not enough. Stuffing a child with milk from the breast in any old fashion as long as the infant survives won't do. A nurturing style of feeding is recommended, because this also fosters *emotion*, the basic unit of communication.

One can think of this further. Take the pleasure of friendship. Friendship has been defined as an association the purpose of which is the very communication between the two people themselves and not to further any other objective. Friendship becomes the high point in communication—communication for its own sake. The personal love that exists between two friends is the basis and reason for the association. So it is that once the survival tasks are taken care of or the time needed to devote to them is minimized, then these elements, originally there for the sake of survival, become taken up for their own sake. As civilization has developed, so the value of *emotion* as a good in itself has become increasingly emphasized.

I said above that speech, art, and music are the outer manifestation or representation of the emotions. The emotions are not visible; as awareness of them begins to grow, so humans begin to represent them. The cave paintings at Lascaux and Altamira and also some of the cave paintings done by Aborigines in Australia—for instance, those in a cave on Groote Eylandt—are no longer signs but representations—but of what? The animals that are painted there are appreciated not just for their worth as a food source but in themselves, for themselves. But this means that something has developed within the human being. We no longer have here just an animal that is driven by the need for food; something has opened out in the personality—a space that is in relation to the animal for its own sake. That something in the personality we call beauty. When those ancestors of ours—about 30,000 years ago—began to draw and paint upon the ceiling of their caves, they were expressing externally the experience of that internal space. Something began to happen in the personality. Means became ends.

I should like here to draw out that remark I just made—that when those ancestors of ours began to draw and paint, they were expressing externally the experience of that internal space. This is not the way I should have put it. I do not agree with Plato's idea that what occurs is a straight transcription onto the outside of what is within, but, rather, the very act of painting is part of the opening of a space, the representational work, and it has an inner and an outer component. As a material representational mark is made, it opens, so to speak, a space beyond it; this "space-beyond" does not come into being until the new gesture, coloured mark, or musical note has been made. We make a great mistake if we think that there is a perfectly formed inner which then becomes expressed in a perfectly formed outer. Following Vico, we can say that the inner is a created reality. The inner is unformed, it is inchoate, it is a seed that contains the adult form but in a compressed, dark, and hidden state. It thrusts, however, like the seed, for growth, for transformation of the formless into form. So when the artist executes his art, the finished visible product is part and parcel of a whole. There is the dark, the hidden, the invisible, the compact and formless and the visible with distinct form, and the two are one: it is one organism. The visible enlightens and the invisible generates power and energy to the visible. The relevance of this becomes clearer in chapter 3.

* * *

I mentioned with a hint of irony that I had come across people who have sex for its own sake rather than to procreate. Under survival mode people join together for the sake of a joint task. So, for instance, Colin Turnbull (1984) says that the BaMbuti, who in politically incorrect days were called pygmies, join together in a group to go hunting. One group holds a big net that stretches for some distance in width while others drive animals into the net. Someone who catches an animal on his own account, as Cephu—one of the tribe—did on one occasion, is banished from the group for some hours as a punishment. So association was for the purpose of a task, but when two people began to associate for their own sakes, as an end in itself, a reality like the space just mentioned began to emerge. We might imagine that at the same time as people began to paint on the ceilings of their caves, so also began a new phenomenon: friendship. We need now to look more carefully into what is occurring in friendship.

* * *

The notion that friendship is its own end and not a means to some other end has been clear within civilized society from the time of Homer. One has only to think of the profound distress of Achilles at the death of his friend, Patroclus, as recorded in the *Iliad* by

Homer. However, I will now go forward some five hundred years and rely on the authority of Cicero (*Laelius: On Friendship*) to back this up:

> Friendship may be defined as a complete identity of feeling about all things in heaven and earth: an identity which is strengthened by mutual goodwill and affection. With the single exception of wisdom, I am inclined to regard it as the greatest of all the gifts the gods have bestowed upon mankind. Some people, I know, give preference to riches, or good health, or power, or public honours. And many rank sensuous pleasures highest of all. But feelings of that kind are something which any animal can experience; and the other items in that list, too, are thoroughly transient and uncertain. They do not hang on our own decisions at all, but are entirely at the mercy of fickle chance. [Cicero, 1984, p. 187]

The words I am concentrating on here are that he refers to *something that any animal can experience*. In another place he says,

> Anyone who wants to allege that a friendship is formed for the sake of advantage seems to me to be doing away with the most attractive things such an association can offer. What we enjoy in a friend is *not* the profit we derive from him, but the affection. Any practical benefit that goes with this affection only gives satisfaction when it is the product of a warm heart. [1984, pp. 204–205]

In another place Cicero says that friendship is not based upon a need in oneself or a deficiency in oneself. To the person who says that friendship should be cultivated for the purpose of mutual utility, he has this to say:

> This would mean that the people who would get the most out of friendship would be those whose wills and bodies are the weakest: helpless women would need its protection more than men, the poor more than the rich, the unfortunate more than those who are considered fortunate. What a peculiar philosophy! People who propound this sort of theory seem to me to be doing nothing less than tearing the very sun out of the heavens. For they are, in fact, depriving life of friendship, which is the noblest and most delightful of all the gifts the gods have given to mankind. [1984, p. 201]

He makes it clear in this that the essence of friendship is annihilated once it is subordinated to a utilitarian need, but it is precisely this that is in the service of survival. Cicero starts this dialogue shortly after his friend, Scipio Africanus, had died, and so he says,

> Consider Africanus, for example. Did he need me? Of course he did not. Nor, for that matter, did I need him. I was attached to him because I admired his fine qualities; and he returned my feelings because he also, on his side, appeared not to have formed too bad an opinion of my own character. [1984, p. 193]

In a general way I think we can say that an association based on utility or engaged in for the sake of sensuous pleasure are therefore a means towards another end, whereas what he is claiming is that friendship is an association engaged in as an end in itself. In contemporary times this issue has received great emphasis from the philosopher John Macmurray—for instance:

> If . . . two people are associated merely for what they can get out of one another it is obviously not a friendship. Two people are friends because they love one another. That is all you can say about it. If the relationship had any other reason for it we should say that one or other of them was pretending friendship from an ulterior motive. This means in effect that friendship is a type of relationship into which people enter as persons with the whole of themselves. To ask David what he expects to get out of his friendship with Jonathan is to insult him by suggesting that he only associates with his friend from self-interest. No doubt he might answer that he gets everything that makes life worth living; but of course what he means is that he gets friendship out of it, which is exactly what he puts into it. [1935, pp. 100–101]

Association as a means to and end is under the hegemony of survival. That great step that mankind took when he and she initiated what we call civilization was separating various human activities from their roots, which had been in the service of survival.

So why am I going on so much about friendship? For the same reason that I am going on about art. It is a fruit of civilization. And civilization opens out something in the human psyche such that elements that were there to serve the needs of survival are now taken up as ends in themselves, and this transformation indicates a change in psychic structure. When trying to define that change, when trying to designate what is there that was not there before or was only there as an unwatered seed, I have said that a space has opened out in the personality. But this is not enough.

Both art and friendship are creations. So yes, call it a space, an emptiness, but one out of which a living creative force emerges. In one of the passages above quoted from Cicero's dialogue on friendship, Macmurray says: "They do not hang on our own decisions at all, but are entirely at the mercy of fickle chance" (1935, p. 187). Therefore he distinguishes between what he refers to as activity that is at the mercy of *fickle chance* and something that depends upon *our own decisions*.

I am stressing friendship because it is the supreme instance where communion between persons is valued for its own sake. It is no longer a means, but an end in itself. And these units of communication in the personality receive their supreme expression in the emotions. There is a link, I believe, between the men and women who started painting in those caves of Altamira and Lascaux and friendship. In both cases the fruit and manifestation of communication is being celebrated. In the case of that primitive art it is the communication between man and nature that is being celebrated but also as a communication to others for its own sake, and in friendship it is communication between one person and another that is being celebrated. And if I am right that the *emotions* are the substance of that communication, then a value upon the *emotions* themselves *for* themselves is being solemnized as something precious, and this receives its supreme expression in friendship. I have had the thought from time to time that the burgeoning of psychotherapy and counselling in the present era is partly a function of the diminution of friendship in our present culture. If this is the case, then I think our culture is a very sick patient.

It is the *emotions* that are the units of this communication, but this is looking at the matter from a social standpoint. How is it from the angle of the individual—you and me? I think there are two dimensions that intersect. One is admiration for a quality that it would be possible to consider in the abstract—like goodness, courage, beauty, truth, or generosity—but these do not exist in the abstract. They are generated from within. They are creations of the individual. In that best-selling book *The Story of Art,* Gombrich, the author, starts with the arresting statement: "There really is no such thing as Art. There are only artists" (1974, p. 4).

So communication at the moment when it becomes an end in itself and not a means is an individual creation. There is a something in the personality that has scooped up the communication that is there as part of the instinctual deposit and made of it something that was not there before. It is that phyllogenetically what was happening is what is happening between one individual and another ontogenetically when they understand each other. There is, then, a source of this creation. There is a creator, and the matter out of which the creation is fashioned are the communicative elements that are originally there in the service of survival.

What about this source, then? You may doubt its existence, and yet out of what womb came the cosmogonies, the myths about the how the world came to be? Almost all societies have had myths about the origin of the world and especially the world of humankind. The one we are all most familiar with is the one recorded in the Book of Genesis, where

> In the beginning God created the heavens and the earth. The earth was without form and void, and darkness was upon the face of the deep; and the Spirit of God was moving over the face of the waters. [Genesis, I, 1]

But how did men come to the idea of a creator fashioning our world if not through projecting onto an outer figure something that they had familiarity with from inside themselves? Nearly all societies had their creation myths. It does not seem to me credible that so many different societies in the earlier days of civilization would have constructed such a mythology unless it corresponded to something that was occurring in the breasts of men and women in many different parts of the world. Incidentally, it is worth noting that in the above passage God does not create out of nothing but, rather,

> The earth was without form and void, and darkness was upon the face of the deep . . . [Genesis, I, 1]

So the idea that God created *ex nihilo,* out of nothing, came as a later theological elaboration. All the creation myths are a creation out of *something,* usually something that is indefinite or formless.

It is like the potter giving form and colour to the shapeless clay. You may remember that I said in chapter 1 that the source of suffering for the individual who approaches a psychoanalyst is that the cause is not known: to become known, a form has to be created out of formlessness.

Yet even so, wherewith this creator, this inner artist? How comes he to be there?

I think this is an unanswerable question. Not so long ago there was the idea of a *homunculus*—a little man, or an observer—within the organism. This idea, called by Daniel Dennett (1993) the *Cartesian Theatre* has been refuted by him. Damasio believes that this, which is a source of consciousness, is to be explained by discovering its biological underpinnings (2000, p. 11); but this tells us how it works; but not the reason for its existence. It is like the question, "Well, how is it that there is a universe?" There is no answer. Big Bang theory and so on only tells us how the form in which matter exists today was yesterday. It does not tell us how it is that there is a universe, only the different formations through which it has passed. So also, I believe, the existence of a creator within the personality cannot be explained. Why was it that this particular animal, *homo sapiens*, was not satisfied with survival? From where did this creative force in him come about? It would have been very surprising if human beings had not puzzled over this down the centuries, and they have. Plato believed that there is in humankind an original endowment, the *innate ideas*, through which we are able to reshape the previous conditions of things. The philosopher Kant also thought that there are innate categories through which we construct our world. Melanie Klein also was in that same tradition of thinking when she believed that within the baby there is an innate idea, however indistinct, of the breast to which it intuitively moves after birth. The philosopher Rudolph Eucken says:

> Thought now becomes both the motive force and the measure of all things: by vigorous self-concentration it discovers in itself an original endowment of eternal truths, then transforms these into postulates, and applies them to the existing condition of things. [1913, p. 235]

I suppose one could crudely divide thinkers into those who have espoused something that has been called "naturalism"—the idea that this creative centre in man is the product of a series of outer identifiable elements that come together to form a creative centre— and those who believe that there is some eternal truth or world soul that is the source of this inner creative energy.

However we attempt to explain it, what we are intent on describing is a spontaneous creative force that wells up within the individual organism, within the individual personality. It is like a spring, a geyser, of pure crystalline water jetting unbeckoned out of the ground. It is this that takes hold of the instinctual elements and forms them into the communicative centre that is our emotional life. Emotions, then, are the communication between one individual and another. We all know in a sort of inchoate way that someone approaches a psychoanalyst or psychotherapist for "emotional problems"—in other words, there is some hiatus in communication. The prime task of the psychoanalyst is, therefore, to restore, repair, or even assist in the installation for the first time of the capacity for communication in the patient who comes to visit him.

So the theory I am developing here is that with the growth of civilization emotional life became an end in itself and, furthermore, this was something that was capable of maturing. The flowering of emotional life happens through deep communication with another person, and in chapter 3 we look at this more closely.

CHAPTER THREE

Emotional development

The question: *How is it that someone who has a problem is able to resolve it through conversation with another?*

"INFANT SORROW

My mother groan'd! my father wept.
Into the dangerous world I leapt:
Helpless, naked, piping loud:
Like a fiend hid in a cloud.

Struggling in my father's hands,
Striving against my swaddling bands,
Bound and weary I thought best
To sulk upon my mother's breast."

William Blake [1972, p. 217]

The place where we have now reached is this: In chapter 1 we posited a solution to the problem that is, I believe, correct as far as it goes. It stressed the way in which a problem is solved if it is highlighted and placed within a pattern governed by a common denominator, and it stressed the way in which a theory can blind the clinician to a knowledge that he possesses inside himself, but it was biased in that the personal element in our question was bypassed. We ended by recognizing this and realizing that we needed to probe further into the nature of the emotions, so in chapter 2 we made our first probe. The conclusion we came up with was that emotions are the elements inside us that are the units of communication. We further said that this communication, as many other activities, was there as an instinctual endowment for the sake of survival, but the advent of civilization marked a momentous change whereby elements that had been a means to an end, a means for survival—such as food and sex—became ends in themselves, but communication itself was the most important of these. We instanced friendship as the supreme instance of communication for its own sake.

I think it is a safe principle that our emotional capital is built up through communication, though this needs some qualification. The communication needs to be of a certain kind for it to build up our emotional capital. I think those who are psychotherapists will have met instances like these. Sophia complains that when she came home from school and ran to her mother and started to cry because her teacher, Mrs Longfellow, had shouted at her, her mother told her not to be such a cry-baby and to go out into the garden and play. On another occasion she was listening to Handel's *Messiah,* and when the choir started to sing the *Hallelujah Chorus,* she jumped up and danced and sang in exuberation. Her mother told her to sit down at once and behave herself. Sophia's mother could not bear intensity of emotion, be it sad or joyful. In Ernest Jones's biography of Freud he gives a short character sketch of Ernst Brücke, Professor of Physiology at Vienna University, under whom Freud studied as a medical student and in whose laboratory he did research for several years:

> The general opinion had him labelled as a cold, purely rational man. What degree of violent force against himself and his emotions he needed to build up this front is revealed by his reaction to the death of his beloved son in 1872. He forbade his family and friends to mention his son's name, put all pictures of him out of sight, and worked even harder than before. [Jones, 1972, pp. 48–49]

These are instances of people—Sophia's mother in one case and Ernst Brücke on the other—who did not have the emotional resources to manage either to assimilate into themselves distressing experiences or to be able to communicate them, either to others or to themselves. So let us take these two people. Let us put to ourselves the hypothesis that they both lack emotional resources. The general psychological view of most of us within the mental health field is that this has arisen because in childhood, in infancy, or even at the foetal stage of development, the mother herself has not had the emotional capacity to manage the clamours, the distress, the appeals for help from this new bundle of burgeoning life with all its needs and turbulent demands.

So we seem to have arrived at the formulation that the capacity to communicate is present to the extent to which the individual him or herself has been communicated to by mother or, in the modern jargon, the primary caregiver. Because what we seem to be saying in the two cases just instanced is that had the mother of Ernst Brücke and Sophia's grandmother been able to enter into communication with their bouncing, clamouring children, then their own capacities to enter into communication with distressing or joyful experiences would have been much greater. The first thing we need to ask ourselves is: is the mother the designated figure who is destined to fulfil this role?

Two questions are of importance here: Can someone else other than the mother enter into communication with the baby in such a way as to help build up the emotional deposit within the infant? Specialists in child health claim that this is the case, and usually in their deliberations they use the term "primary caregiver" rather than mother. This debate can obviously only apply to infants after birth because at the foetal stage of development there would seem to be little doubt that if there is communication to the baby then the communicative agent will be the mother, although surrogate motherhood raises new questions.

* * *

When the foetus is wrestling around inside the womb, it would seem that the mother is the person who is in communication with either the stormy or tranquil creature within. Before we go on, it is worth considering whether the foetus in the womb does receive communications from the mother. I think that there is considerable evidence that there is such communication between mother and baby. For instance, at the Fells Institute in the United States a number of pregnant mothers were being closely observed, and while this was happening, the husband of one mother became psychotic and tried to kill her. The foetal movements inside the mother increased tenfold and continued so for some time subsequent to this incident. Also some psychoanalysts have observed transference phenomena that seems to date from this early period of intrauterine life. What happens in the womb seems to me so important that I thought I'd give a clinical example that illustrates how what happens in the womb leaves an imprint upon later post-natal life that can stretch right into adulthood.

This clinical vignette comes from an unpublished paper written by a colleague in America who was working in a psychiatric unit. He is an analyst who has written a certain amount on the significance of the foetal stage of development and the way this affects subsequent emotional behaviour in adulthood. In the first part of the paper he runs through some of the theorists to show how later in their clinical lives they attended more and more to the importance of the foetal stage of development. He mentions Melanie Klein in this regard, and also Bion. He also mentions an association in Switzerland that is devoted to the study of the psychological correlates of the foetal stage of development. He then gives a clinical example taken from when he was acting as consultant in the psychiatric unit, which was run along therapeutic community lines:

> The patient was a woman of 35 who had already been referred to us some months previously by one of the consulting psychiatrists of a large mental hospital in the hope that inpatient psychoanalytic psychotherapy might prove to be of more help than other forms of treatment attempted until then. Her first stay with us lasted only a fortnight because on the fourteenth day she made a suicidal gesture that aroused so much anxiety in the staff that we asked the referring hospital to take her back on the grounds that her life would be at risk if she remained with us any longer. With the knowledge and approval of the referring consultant she subsequently wrote to us several times begging us on the grounds of humanity to give her a second chance, and eventually we agreed to do this.

Her second admission was preceded by a letter from the referring consultant saying she had been anorexic. We found this to
be indeed so, and within a few days of her arrival her vomit-
ing and failure to eat became sufficiently great for the nursing
staff to supply her with a special diet that she could keep down
and to organize a rota of patients and nurses who would help
her with it and make sure she ate it. This did not augur well
for the patient's future appetite for psychotherapy and was
interpreted to her as expressing her ambivalence towards it. In
addition to the anxieties produced by the anorexia itself, the
patient began to create in the nursing staff a new kind of stress
and frustration. She did this by hardly relating to anyone at all,
patients or nurses, and keeping most of the time to her own
room. Completely isolated, she lived in a world of her own,
and this in itself put quite a strain on the nurses and on the
other patients. In the course of this anorexic phase the patient
developed a series of abundant nose-bleeds, one after the other.
These became sufficiently severe—35 in three days—for us to
eventually to send her to the neighbouring general hospital
for an opinion. The doctor who examined her there reported
that he'd seen traces in her nasal cavities that suggested self-
inflicted injuries to the mucous membrane, but he could not be
certain about it. I questioned the patient about this in the next
session. She denied having done anything to herself. She then
went on to say, in a half-amused, half self-conscious sort of way,
that during the nose-bleeds she had been swallowing her own
blood, and that one of the nurses who was attending her at the
time had caught her doing this and had jokingly said to another
patient who happened to be standing by: "Look at Dracula's
daughter having her meal." Swallowing her own blood, the patient continued, gave her a feeling of living off herself, and with
a half-apologetic smile she explained that it was easier to do
this than to attack other people. Her expression then changed,
and in a more serious, almost factual manner she concluded by
saying that when swallowing her blood, she derived additional
comfort from weaving an imaginary cocoon around herself;
she showed me what she meant by tracing an imaginary spiral
that started at her head and went round towards her feet and
back. She had already told me about this weaving of cocoons

in the course of her admission but appeared to have forgotten it. What she had said then was that the cocoon was the only place where she could feel really safe and completely herself, and it would be damaging if the cocoon were to be broken. She had also previously told me that she felt safer in the consulting-room than in the rest of the hospital, where she claimed that everyone had got it in for her. I had said that the cocoon seemed represented by the consulting-room and myself, and she had agreed with this. Her clinging to this safe cocoon aspect of her perception of me had clearly been a defence against her fear of experiencing me as an angry father who'd want to break the cocoon open. But that particular interpretation was met with a vigorous denial.

As this earlier cocoon material was now reappearing in a context that contained references to blood meals and living off her own blood because it is easier to do this than to attack other people and, by implication, living off theirs, there seemed to me some grounds for interpreting this not only within the transference but also in such a way as to do justice towards what appeared to be the full force of the aggressivity involved. I was, of course, aware that, unlike the legendary vampire, the foetus does not obtain its blood by biting or sucking, but what I was basing myself on here was the notion that I mentioned earlier—namely, that the foetus, too, like the vampire, can be said to live off blood silently, unseen, and in the dark. It seemed to me justified, therefore, to look upon this new presentation of the cocoon material as pointing to the existence of a foetal blood-consuming parasitical and very aggressive form of transference, the aggressivity of which the patient presumably dealt with between sessions by deflecting it on herself and living off her own blood instead of that of others. My interpretation was as follows: I told the patient that when she was united with me in what she felt to be the cocoon of my office, the foetus part of herself was to some extent able to live off the blood of words, care, and attention and thus feel relatively safe. But when the end of the session caused the cocoon to be broken and the umbilical link with me to be severed, the life-and-death quality of her foetal dependence on me made it imperative that she immediately find some other body to sustain her. When it came to other people, however, she was no longer quite as sure of herself or of them as she was of me. She distrusted them and herself with them. She feared that if she directed at them the full force of her foetal greed and craving, it might either destroy them or cause them to retaliate. Rather than then attack these other people in this way, she found it easier between sessions to get from her own body the blood that she could not get from me. I thus tried to convey to her that I thought she was using me not only as a cocoon or a safe place to be in, but also as a prenatal mother-type of object on which she could exercise the aggressive as well as the libidinal components of her un-resolved prenatal drive. I added that her anorexia could well express her wish to revert to an umbilical intrauterine kind of feeding. The patient appeared to have taken in what I had said, but she made no reply.

Within two days of that particular session she not only began to eat normally, but she also began to make more contact with other people, even if in a rather greedy, demanding, and clumsy sort of way. The nurses immediately perceived the change, and they all said they much preferred this new and more open kind of demandingness to the one in which the patient had with-drawn into herself and hardly related to them at all. My reading of the change at the time was that if my comments had played any part in bringing it about, it was perhaps because the patient now felt her prenatal cravings to be sufficiently understood for her not to have to sort them out in order to draw attention to them, and that she was now functioning and relating at a more postnatal level something to which the nurses could more eas-ily respond. What followed, however, was to make me come to the conclusion that a large part of the prenatal repression had in fact continued to operate and at a level that was perhaps even deeper than I had realized at that time. I had previously thought that the patient was simply trying to use me as a pre-natal mother sort of object, but there now seemed to be grounds for thinking that the real prenatal mother object was the hospi-tal community, and that as far as I was concerned she expected me to carry out for her in relatedness to this community a role similar to that which the placenta performs for the unborn child in helping it relate to the mother's body.

* * *

I have gone into some length about the foetal stage of development to highlight the fact that there is evidence of communication at this very early stage. Some years ago I was treating a woman who knew that her mother had not wanted her when she found she was pregnant; she came to me for over-eating and also for smoking nonstop most of the day. This is how things progressed.

> She was smoking a cigarette outside just before the session began. She said to herself, "*I will not tell, Neville*", but of course she did tell me, and that is how I knew. So I observed that there were two conflicting desires in her: one that said, "*Don't tell Neville*", and the other, which does tell me. I elaborated the matter and said that it seemed that there was one desire that was to communicate and give herself fully and be fully present to me and another that smothered that desire. She listened to me and replied thus:

> "I believe that a mother communicates what she feels to her unborn foetus. I think when I came along as an unwanted pregnancy, my *mother hated it and that communicated itself to me . . .*"

> So I said,

> "and that this hatred is still in you, smothering the desire to live, to communicate fully, to give of yourself. It's the voice that says inside you '*Don't tell Neville*'."

and the session carried on upon those lines.

In his later life, as demonstrated in various statements at seminars, Bion gave more and more weight to the foetal stage of development. He said at a seminar in New York:

> Suppose the foetus arrives at what the obstetricians call "full term". Does the foetus have to be born before it has a personality or a mind? Conversely, does man have a mind? I see no reason to doubt that the full-term foetus has a personality. It seems to me to be gratuitously non-sensical to suppose that the

physical fact of birth is something which creates a personality which was not in existence before then. [Bion, 1980, p. 22]

So I put my weight behind the view that the mother is in communication with the foetus in her womb and that the nature of this communion between the mother and her unborn child affects the emotional state of the infant at the time of birth. There are two points here: that the nature of the communication affects the emotional constitution first of the foetus and then of the infant, and that there is communication at the nonverbal level.

I once had this experience.

A woman was on the couch in an analytic session when I was gripped by a violent feeling. "Get out of here. I don't want you here in this room." That was the violent feeling that suddenly welled up in me. You will, I hope, be glad to hear that I did not act on this feeling either in word or in act. A moment later the patient said,

"When I was five months pregnant, my mother nearly miscarried. I think she wanted to get rid of me."

* * *

I want now to pass back to the question of whether, once the infant is born, responsive communication is possible from a figure other than the mother. The person who has argued for the view that the only figure capable of providing such communication being the mother is Anthony Storr, and the person who has argued against it is Jonathan Gathorne-Hardy.

So one aspect of the problem is, "Can someone else other than the mother provide the communication that is necessary for the infant's development of the emotional deposit within?" The other is, "Does this communication need to occur in infancy?" "If it does not occur in infancy, is it too late?" I think many of us are familiar with the theory of *critical periods* first discovered and elaborated by the ethologist Konrad Lorenz. He discovered, for instance, that a duckling needed to swim within between 14 and 17 hours after birth; if it did not do so, then it would never be able to swim. The lost opportunity became irrecoverable. So does the laying down of an emotional deposit have to occur within a particular period in infancy, and if it does not happen in that period, then is it too late? Can it occur later in life? If the development of the emotional deposit depends critically upon the right type of communication from the mother or mother substitute at a period of early infancy, then any later attempts to make good this deficiency will be doomed to failure. Is this correct? What does all our psychoanalytic and psychotherapeutic experience teach us in this regard?

There is certainly a very strong view that what happens emotionally in infancy is crucial and that damage done at this stage either cannot be repaired or can only be repaired with great difficulty, yet I think it is probably implied in a different way. The idea that there can be relationships in later life that are either traumatizing to the individual or, on the other hand, restorative is not very strongly established in the mental health field. As always, though, there are exceptions: Bruno Bettelheim thought that there could be intense experiences in later life that could change someone's emotional constitution. I consider in chapter 6 the way in which traumatic experiences may enable the personality to reorganize a pattern set down in childhood. To glimpse it briefly now we may have to go outside the official field to find an alternative view. What comes powerfully to my mind is the way in which in *Crime and Punishment* Dostoyevsky's character Raskolnikov was restored to sanity through the joint experience of imprisonment in Siberia combined with Sonia's love for him. This is, of course, a novel, but no doubt based on the author's personal experience of being imprisoned in Siberia. However, there are also other examples: that of Caryll Houselander, Marion Milner, and, of course, the testimony of many people who have changed emotionally as a consequence of psychoanalysis or psychotherapy. Caryll Houselander, in the introduction to her book *Guilt*, says that she was what she called an ego-neurotic, but that she managed to cure herself of it, and she was offering the book to help fellow sufferers. She describes the condition thus:

> Ego-neurotics often find it impossible to realize that they can be happy, that they can have a zest for life, know the fullness of joy, and even add to the sum total of life-giving love in the world themselves. The ego-neurotic is usually lonely, he finds it difficult to explain his unhappiness; when put into words it sounds trivial, he finds it difficult to find a sympathetic listener,

or one who could help even if he did listen. [Houselander, 1952]

She goes on the make it plain that it is possible in adult life to change this isolated condition. What she is describing are people whose emotional resources are stunted, but it is clear from her books that she developed an enormous capacity to love and embrace the pains of life, and this occurred for her in later life. In a similar way in her two books *An Experiment in Leisure* and *A Life of One's Own* Marion Milner, writing under the name Joanna Field (1987a, 1987b), describes how she changed emotionally. These people testify to profound changes that came to them in later life. I think one would have to argue from their case histories that our emotional direction is not finalized in childhood.

You will understand why I am bringing this matter up. Can a conversation with someone who is not the mother and at a later stage of life enrich the emotional deposit?—water the seed or repair the damage? Our thesis is that it is communication itself that fertilizes the emotional ovum inside someone. We who are psychoanalysts or psychotherapists have a strong disposition to believe that communication in adulthood is capable of fertilizing the emotional potential in our patients or clients: our professional livelihood depends upon it. We almost take it for granted that this strange conversation that we engage in day-in, day-out is capable of increasing the emotional capital in our client. I think we also have the view that we are doing something that should have been done in childhood by the mother, by the father, or by substitutes for these, though I believe that this assumption can subtly interfere with the therapist's work.

So we have two assumptions to look into in this chapter. Is the mother's role not only to feed her baby, but also to enter into communication with it? I want to turn now to the research that has been done on attachment,[1] though with a caution: enthusiasms for new fields of research should not overwhelm us into thinking that this will show us the reality of emotional life. New fields, like attachment theory and neuroscience, are highlighted because they have been neglected, but if they are pursued in some absolute sense, then they become seductresses. They are not at the core of communication, of inner and outer relationships, of emotional life. They tells us something about the how of things, but not about the thing itself. If taken as primary instead of secondary, they lead us into what Eckhart called *the root of all fallacy* (Kelley, 1977, p. 42). What we seem to keep avoiding so desperately is what is truly primary. We will chase up any avenue rather than the one that will take us to our destination.

* * *

As many of us know, the pioneer in the field of attachment behaviour was John Bowlby. As he is so important, I will give a small résumé of his life (Bowlby's biography has been written by Jeremy Holmes, 1993). John Bowlby was born in 1907; he was one of six children. He was brought up in the way that was typical for someone born into the English upper-middle class. He was largely reared by nannies and governesses. His mother supervised the nursery but was not closely involved. His father, Sir Anthony Bowlby, was the King's surgeon and had been knighted for his role. John's elder brother, Tony, inherited the title when his father died in 1929. John was shipped off to prep school when he was 7; he then went as a naval cadet to Dartmouth, but, at the finish of his schooling there, he decided not to follow a naval career: he went instead to Cambridge to study medicine. During this time he worked in a school that was an offshoot of A. S. Neill's Summerhill, and it was here that he first posited that delinquency arose from alienation from the mother at an early age. He finished his medical training at University College London. He started his training in psychoanalysis and had his personal analysis with Joan Riviere, who was one of Melanie Klein's followers. He qualified as an analyst in 1937. He was supervised by Melanie Klein in a child case that he treated, but he believed that she attributed too much to phantasy and not enough to real factors in the mother's relation with her child. Thus began a rift between Bowlby and the Kleinians that remained for the rest of his long life. He worked in the London Child Guidance Clinic and then at the Tavistock, where he stayed until the time of his death in 1995.

When I was at the Tavistock, up on the fourth floor in the Adult Department, in the 1970s and 1980s, he had his room further down the corridor from mine, we exchanged greetings as we passed each other, and we also used to meet at that male venue—the urinal. When I became involved in the psychotherapeutic treatment of the mentally handicapped, I once asked him at this latter venue whether the attachment behaviour of a mentally handicapped child was different from that of a normal child. He said he knew of no differences in their attachment behaviour. This answer of his surprised me, and he gave it in a disavowed tone that was very familiar to me. Whether the venue prejudiced his answer I cannot say, but it was a surprise to me. He was quintessentially English and answered me in that somewhat stylized manner, as if he were giving orders to a subordinate lieutenant in the army. He was part of the English Establishment, and his connections helped a great deal in making his researches into the effects of maternal deprivation reach ears that could be influential. In fact it was Bowlby's influence that revolutionized hospital child care throughout Britain and beyond.

Bob Gosling, who was Chairman of the Tavistock from 1970 to 1980, once related an incident that does Bowlby credit. When Gosling was elected as Chairman, the other contender for the position was Bowlby, but Bob had thought that Bowlby had not really wanted the position because he had, at the time, so many other commitments—especially in the United States, which he was visiting at the time. So Gosling was elected Chairman of the Tavistock, and Bowlby became his right-hand man and helped him greatly in his role. It was only years later that Ursula, Bowlby's wife, told Bob that John had been bitterly disappointed not to be elected Chairman of the Tavistock. Bob told me that Bowlby never showed a hint of this disappointment—there was never a trace of sulkiness, and he always assisted Bob in every way he could. He was an English gentleman to his fingertips.

Although he was opposed to Melanie Klein's emphasis on the internal at the expense of the external, as he saw it, I never sensed that he was bitter about it.

The kernel of Bowlby's theory is that a child's separation from its mother in its early years has a very damaging effect on the child's mental health. The classic case was of a mother who had to go off into hospital when her child was two years old, and so the child lost her mother for two or three weeks or longer, and this had a very serious effect on the child and affected the mental life and conduct of the child and later the adult, and this could last for the whole of a long life. I tried once to help a man in psychotherapy whose elder brother at the age of five had fallen from the balcony of their third-floor flat and been killed. This happened when my patient was two. You can imagine the effect of this on the parents. My patient lost his mother, not to a hospital, but to a dark cloud of grief. It was clear to me that his alcoholism, his drug addiction, and his enormous difficulty in commitment had their source in this disaster that had occurred in his childhood. He found it very difficult to assimilate the fact that a tragedy when he was aged two could have such effects right through a long life. In his early researches Bowlby instanced cases where the effects on the mental life of the individual were due to a mother's physical absence from her baby, but later he emphasized that emotional absence could also have extremely deleterious effects. This personal example of mine would fall into the latter category.

Initially Bowlby claimed that maternal deprivation produced physical, intellectual, behavioural, and emotional damage. Researchers in the school of Bowlby since his time have demonstrated that intellectual and physical disadvantage are usually unimpaired by maternal deprivation, but emotional development is strangled. So, for instance, Peter Hobson says that children of borderline mothers could succeed in nonsocial tasks as well as children of normal mothers, but they functioned much less well in any exercises that involved social sharing (Hobson, 2002, p. 135). These findings of more recent researchers support my hypothesis that emotions are the units of communication between people. In other words, if a mother communicates well with her baby, it sets in train a learning schedule that carries through into relations not only with the mother, but with other people also. The way I see it, the potential for communication is there in the infant, and what stirs it into action is the communicative engagement of the mother with her baby. This is an instance of what I referred to in chapter 1 when I said that higher principles are able to encompass a wide range of developmental models. This would be an example of one of them—that communication of a particular kind generates the capacity to communicate. In fact, therefore, it assists in the creation of a person—that the individual develops a unified centre instead of remaining an unintegrated aggregate. This is the very centre of what I want to convey here, and I come back to it more emphatically in subsequent chapters. Bowlby put in with a broad brush the general hypothesis that as a result of maternal deprivation people are affected in their behaviour, intellect, and physical deportment. Later researchers have defined this more accurately and have pin-pointed the place of maximum damage and separated this from other behavioural and mental arenas that are less affected. I believe that Bowlby has been criticized too severely for his inaccuracies. The social pioneer sounds the alarm signal and demonstrates the direction of the journey; it is the job of later scientists to refine the matter with greater precision, and one would hope that they would be grateful to their guide, who first directed them on their journey.

I want to put in an aside here. I say an aside not to indicate the degree of its importance but, rather, its diversion from the main argument that is here being pursued. I will quote again therefore the statement that I have just made:

> If a mother communicates well with her baby, it sets in train a learning schedule that carries through into relations not only with the mother, but with other people also. . . .

This is a particular piece of learning theory. Well, what is learn-ing theory doing in a psychoanalytic text? I think such a question belies a terrible misunderstanding of what psychoanalysis is. Psy-choanalysis is not a body of knowledge: rather, it is a psychological enquiry; an investigation of this kind may reveal that the psycho-logical problem may be due to a failure in learning, a neurological disorder, or a distorted perception. This perspective broadens our horizons immeasurably. I say this with some emphasis as I saw in a recent paper by quite a well-known analyst where psychoanaly-sis being defined as "a body of knowledge about the mind". Thus ends the aside.

There has been such a huge amount of research into infant development that I could not, even if I were able, sketch even the barest outline, and I shall not attempt it. I want, instead, to take what I believe is one of the key issues that has been uncovered, in particular by Peter Hobson and his associates. I will give you a key quote from his very good book:

> The person who is free to evaluate attachments is able to assimilate and *think about* her own past experiences in rela-tionships, even when these have been unsatisfactory. She has

mental space to relate to her own relations with others. She can reflect on her own feelings and impulses and can forgive and tolerate her own shortcomings. So, too, she has space to relate to her own baby as an independent and separate person and to be sensitive to her baby's states of mind in such a way that the baby is likely to become securely attached. [Hobson, 2002, p. 178]

Therefore when the mother is able to embrace her own experiences and contain them within the perimeter of her own individual person, then she is able to relate to her baby *as she is*. She is able to see her baby in his own individual shape and form and relate to him as such. Therefore the condition that allows mother to see her baby *as she is* is her own self-awareness, and this in itself is the product of an act in which her own past is embraced. I don't want us all to nod and say "Yes, yes" and complacently go to sleep. To elucidate this self-awareness, we need to ask, then, what the state is of those other mothers Hobson talks about who were not self-aware. He refers to those who are not self-aware as being *enmeshed,* and this is the word favoured by those who have made researches into attachment behaviour: "The person who is enmeshed appears to have been unable to accomplish a full separation from her early caregivers", says Hobson (2002, p. 179). It seems that a feature of this state is an inability to create the other as a figure in the mind. When you are enmeshed with another, then you cannot create the other as a figure in your own mind. The enmeshed state is also a feature of autism, or vice versa. Two things need to be said about this.

It seems that frequently when a certain clinical syndrome is identified clearly in a few cases, then traces of the same condition begin to be seen to exist more widely. One can see this in the development of Frances Tustin's thought. She first observed the condition in the young boy, John, whom she treated (Tustin, 1972); she then began to see this condition more widely in other patients, and the title of her third book is a résumé of this position: *Autistic Barriers in Neurotic Patients* (Tustin, 1986). However, I think this phenomenon can be considered on an even wider scale than this. Perhaps I can articulate my viewpoint best by quoting a paragraph in a letter I wrote to Peter Hobson after he had published his first book, *Autism and the Development of Mind* (1993):

Now for a mad thought: when you say on page four that the autistic person does not perceive persons as a special class of things, I thought this is a living parody of those psychologists and philosophers who view the world of people as if there were no difference between them and things. The mad thought is: is it truly a parody, or is it possible that a social disease has its reflected counterpart in an actual living clinical abnormality? An abnormality that would not exist were it not for the social disease, and that the cure of the individual abnormality is impossible without healing the social disease? How could a social disease transmit into an individual psychological abnormality? Or could it be that when the autistic condition is first articulated by Kanner, it is on his part an act of prophecy?

I will just mention that in his reply Peter said that he thought the connection was more likely to be just analogical, not causal. Yet I am not quite prepared to give up my mad thought. I somehow want to hold on to the possibility that this may be so: that what we see in a particular clinical syndrome is a magnification on a small scale of a cultural disease that is very widespread. If this is true, then the significance for the clinician is enormous, because it would very much alter the vertex—to use Bion's phrase—from which he views the phenomena he encounters in his consulting-room. If *enmeshment* is integral to autism and if this condition is part and parcel of the culture, then its transmission from culture to mothers to babies can be a very real concern. It would mean that to combat this condition a battle needs to be conducted on three fronts: against a disease in the culture, against its presence in mothers, and against in its presence in babies.

I want to dwell a bit more on what I have called "cultural diseases". The idea that the patient who comes to visit us in our consulting-room is crazy and that we represent, as psychiatrists or psychoanalysts or psychotherapists, the society that is sane is a very dangerous assumption. The patient's complaint could be precisely against a mad element in our society. As Erich Fromm said, there can be not only a *folie à deux* but also a *folie à millions* (1972, p. 16); this was the case in Nazi Germany, but we should not sit back in comfort and think that such madness occurred only in one isolated instance of recent history. One only has to think of the craziness of the Allied powers in their handling of their victory over Germany in 1918, of the violent oppression that occurred in Stalinist Russia, of the madness that occurred in China under Mao Tse-Tung (which has been well documented in Jung Chang's *Wild Swans*, 1991), the behaviour of the Taliban in their destruction of the Buddhist statues that Shahid Najeeb has lectured upon. But our own society is also riddled with madnesses. I said in chapter 2 that I suspect that there is much less friendship in our society today than there was a hundred years ago, and that individual persons are more used for utilitarian purposes proportionally than they were a century ago. There are also subcultures within our society that are mad. A great deal has been written about the consumerism and economic rationalism that undermine the creative urges in all of us, undermine those intuitions founded on something very sane. Certain aspects of madness are not easy to detect, but there have nearly always been prophets a long way ahead of their time who have sniffed out the first beginnings of a cultural disease. Max Weber, the sociologist, died in 1920, but already then he was predicting the growth of bureaucracy in modern society with its treatment of people as things—cogs in a machine. This is now so much the very air we breathe that we have come to believe that what is mad is sane. For instance, many academics complain that education is at a premium in the universities: that instead of education, students today are being trained to become technocrats in an increasingly technocratic society; but already in 1941 Alfred North Whitehead was saying that perhaps universities were ceasing to be the vehicles and agents of education, and that some new institution would be formed to fulfil the role.

The patient who comes to our consulting-room is frequently clamouring against these social forces that he or she finds difficult to resist. The patient may be the sane one, and it is his or her very sanity that needs to be strengthened sufficiently to stand up against an outer madness. Such madness is also implanted into the subculture, including psychoanalytic institutes and also psychotherapeutic associations. There is at the moment much disquiet that many people are eschewing these institutions. We need to consider that they may perceive, albeit unconsciously, something that is against the emotional health of the individual person. One also needs to consider that societies are constantly changing, and that it is sometimes patients—perhaps patients even more than other members of the community—who point out the direction of these changes. As therapists, we may be imposing upon them our cherished ideas of sanity, which belong to an era that is passing, if it has not already passed. The mad thought, though, is that when a clinical entity is seen and described for the first time, it is a reflection of what is in the culture. This is the first point I want to make.

The second is that what applies to mothers and babies may also apply in adult relationships more generally. Hobson, reflecting on Fonagy, Steele, and Steele's (1991) finding in a study of pregnant mothers that 75% of secure mothers had securely attached children whereas 73% of enmeshed mothers had insecurely attached children, has this to say: "These are remarkable findings. They make one wonder whether the qualities of a person's thinking about childhood might be important not only for parent–child interactions, but also for adult intimate relationships" (Hobson, 2002, p. 156).

So the question here is: is what is true of mothers with their infants also true of what happens between one adult and another? This brings us back to the point made earlier. Is this emotional development confined to a *critical period* in infancy, or can it happen later in life? Can an adult receive from another adult what the infant receives or should have received from its mother?

I am working now on the hypothesis that this is possible: that if an adult gives to another adult the same ingredient that a mother gives to her child, then the one to whom that is given grows in his or her constructive development. I am going, then, on the hypotheses

1. that there is *not* a *critical period* for the establishment of emotional confidence;
2. that the other person need not be the mother but can be any concerned adult.

And, of course, behind these two hypotheses is the view that "emotional capital" is built up through a particular form of communication with another.

What I now posit is that emotional growth occurs through communication with a person. What do I mean by this—surely we are all persons? In chapter 5 I cover briefly some of the ideas of the neurologist Antonio Damasio, but I mention that these views are not well internalized in me—that I am, to some extent, in the role of a parrot when I talk of them. I have quoted before that trenchant statement of Dostoyevsky's:

> Talk rot by all means, but do it your own way, and I'll be ready to kiss you for it. For to talk nonsense in your own way is a damn sight better than talking sense in someone else's; in the first case, you're a man; in the second you're nothing but a magpie. [1978, p. 219]

What is the difference between information or an idea that has been internalized and one that is than purely ingested? The difference between human talk and magpie talk? The latter suggests that it is possible for something to be in me, but very much as a foreign body—that is, that there are two ways in which something can be in my personality: either as a piece of extraneous matter or as something that has become part of me. The obvious analogy is the digestive system, where a piece of food is broken down and becomes part of the body—but what is the mental correlate of this digestive system? It is the human capacity to create. A bit of extraneous matter only becomes me through an act of creation. The creative force within me is like the digestive juices. Something is made part of me through an inner creative act. It was well understood at one time that human beings are not fulfilled if they do not create. The historian Arthur Bryant says: "Man is, by nature, a producer or creator as well as a consumer, and unless the instinct to create and produce implanted in him by nature is satisfied, he will, to a greater or lesser degree, be an unsatisfactory and discontented being" (Bryant, 1969, p. 268); a page later he continues: "If man is not given the opportunity to create, he will, in his unconscious frustration, destroy" (p. 269).

The culture of consumerism deadens that *instinct to create*. The importance of this is enormous, because all relationships, but especially friendship, are a created reality. We need to link what we are saying here with the point stressed in chapter 3: that the emotions, the *space-between*, is a creation. In the attachment studies that I have read I have not seen much attention given to the transition from a glue-like bondage or *enmeshed* state, as it is usually called, to one where a space has been created. I have quoted above Fonagy, Steele, and Steele's (1991) study showing that mothers who are able to reflect on their own childhood experience have a much higher percentage of secure children than *enmeshed* mothers, but quite how someone moves from the *enmeshed* state to the *space-between* state has not, as far as I know, been given much attention in the research. I believe that research into this transition would deepen our understanding of the difference between a created relationship as opposed to an addictive one. I have myself given much thought to this matter, and the way I work clinically, especially in recent years, has been influenced by those thoughts. I think the transition in the patient or client can take place only if the right mental stance is present in the therapist. What is certain is that the imposition of a received theory will act as a constraint and prevent the creative act in the other.

No one can *make* me perform an inner creative act. By its very definition it is something that occurs freely inside me. Compulsion and the act of creation are mutually exclusive. There are very few creative people in societies governed by tyrants. In Stalinist Russia, for instance, there were a few heroes—Solzhenitsyn, Boris Pasternak, Anna Akhmatova—who were creative despite severe penalties for being so. A tyrannical society that tries to reduce its people into slave-like compliance is, by its very charter, savagely against that creativity that is the hallmark of someone with a mind of his or her own. This has always been so, whether we are thinking of the military regime of ancient Sparta, the theocratic state in Geneva under Calvin's draconian regime in the sixteenth century, or the dictatorship of Hitler over the German people 65 years ago. The terror of such tyrannies pulverizes the population into a collectivity of living corpses. Of course what we see in such instances is tyranny in concentrated form, but it is present to some extent in all societies, including our own, and there are also within any society subcultures that are freer and others that are more tyrannical. It will always, then, be an emotional struggle for a person in any society to achieve personhood.

There are two ways in which an individual is put together. Either the different parts are glued together helter-skelter, and then that person has no inner power but is subject to the pressures that both surround him and are in him; there is no inner resource with which to edit, process, and take in what conforms to his own character and to reject what is foreign. Such an individual has what Bion described as *"an improvisation of a personality"* or *"an improvisation of fragments"* (Bion, 1992, p. 74) or what Winnicott called a *false self* (Winnicott, 1965, pp. 140–152). The other way is when an inner essence has created all these fragments into its own developing form. In the former case there is no true unity but, rather, an aggregate, whereas in the latter there is a unity based on an inner coherence. These two different ways in which an entity is structured exist not only at the human level: they go right down to the basic material level. A distinction has been made by scientists between individual entities and compounds on the one side and aggregates on the other. Charles Birch, whom we have already met, defines an aggregate as "a grouping of entities that does not lead to a higher order of unified experience" (1995, p. 80). He goes on to say that a molecule is a compound, but a rock is an aggregate. So this difference in composition that we are referring to in the human being is something that can be seen right through the fabric of the universe.

In the case of an individual or compound, the parts are put together not on the basis of an incongruous contiguity, but according to the developing form. This latter individual is a self-creation: the name for such an individual is "a person". In the service of psychological accuracy I believe that the term "person" should be reserved for an individual who is created according to such a developing form. We might also categorize these two modes of being as insane as opposed to sane, or mad as opposed to healthy. The fact that the mad or insane may be very widespread and even dominant in the culture should not deter us from calling it insane. We need to remember Erich Fromm's caution that there can be a *folie à millions* (1972, p. 16).

So this is the inner state of affairs. But is there any outer way that favours the creation of a person? As we have already said, any form of tyranny or constraint prevents it or makes it extremely difficult to achieve. It may sound from this that I am referring just to well-known tyrannical societies, but there can be subtle tyrannical subcultures. My own belief is that the reason for the present crisis in psychoanalysis is that its institutional forms are, at present, such a subculture.

So we know the conditions that hinder such a creation. What, then, are the conditions that favour it? Quite simply it is to be in the presence of a person. A person is by definition one that has gathered all parts of him/herself into a coherent whole. Negatively this means that no parts are discharged out of herself and positively that parts that are discharged at her are not batted back but returned in personal transformed form. The presence of the person is generative for the other to create his or her own person. Communication from a person, a being who is unified, is different in essence from communication from an individual who is an aggregate. The former leads to an internal representational change; the latter to an external accommodation with an inner state of disunity.

In this chapter we have been largely laying down some familiar groundwork. In the next two chapters we shall get down to the heart of the business.

NOTE

1. I should like to thank Dr Rachel Falk for her invaluable help in teaching this reluctant school-child the two-times table of attachment theory.

CHAPTER FOUR

Communication and emotion

The question: *How is it that someone who has a problem is able to resolve it through conversation with another?*

"Toda a benção que nâo é aceite, transforma-se numa mald-içâo." [Every blessing that is not accepted becomes a curse.]

Paulo Coelho [1966, p. 66]

We have put to ourselves this question. In chapter 1 we put forward the idea that the solution to a problem lies in the ability to place it within a theoretical schema into which it fits, plus the realization that if the explanatory model being used is wrong, it is counterproductive because it stops us getting in touch with what we know inside ourselves. We ended by saying that this is not enough in itself because it is too impersonal. In chapter 2 we tried to understand emotions, and we came to the conclusion that they are the basic units of communication. In chapter 3 we tried to understand what we might call the developmental history of the emotions and the agents through which they are fostered in us and the conditions that make their development possible. Now I want to look in detail at the way the emotions are fostered through conversation.

We need first to go back to our formulation of what a problem is. You will probably remember my saying that the core of the problem is that we do not know the reason for it, and this led me to suggest that through relating one element to others in a pattern and finding a common denominator what was unknown becomes known—but, as I have just said, this is considering that the cause of distress can be considered quite impersonally.

In chapter 2 we said that the emotions are the basic units, the building-blocks, of communication; I want to stress here that failure in communication is a source of distress. There are two aspects to failure in communication—failure because I do not have the same level of emotional equipment as the person with whom I am engaging and failure because the one I am engaging with does not have the same level of emotional equipment as myself.

I will begin by taking the first of these two: Joanna, with insufficient emotional resources, experiences problems with which she is unable to deal. She capitulates whenever her husband castigates her, she gets into rages with her younger daughter, she is depressed. She goes to see her GP, who refers her to Mrs Shuttlehen, a well-known psychotherapist in the district. In the assessment Mrs Shuttlehen realizes that Joanna is terrified of death, and this saps her vitality, leading her to being depressed. Now, for the moment, we are going to assume that Joanna's emotional resources are smaller than Mrs Shuttlehen's. After all, Mrs Shuttlehen is in the role of psychotherapist: emotions are her stock in trade, just as quadratic equations are for a mathematician or precious stones for a jeweller. So she has knowledge of emotions: yet we need to be careful. She has read the books, she knows the language of emotions but . . . does she have the emotions that the language credits her with? The fact that she has the status does not mean that she has the goods. There is no exam that can test it, as would be the case with a mathematician being tested to see whether she is able to solve quadratic equations; no test such as we could give to a jeweller to see whether she can distinguish between real diamonds and fake ones, because the emotions are not visible. There are accompanying signs—tears when someone is sad, a loud voice when someone is angry, and so on—but these are not the emotions themselves, as we have said; and, as we know, there can be crocodile tears, and an actor can shout loudly but not be angry. The core of anger or sadness is in an invisible activity, so how would one test for it? Psychotherapy institutes try to guarantee the unobstructed availability of emotions in the psychotherapist by insisting that candidates have therapy or psychoanalysis themselves, but, of course, this is no guarantee. If the psychotherapist conducting the therapy is emotionally impoverished but does not know it, then this will not guarantee that the patient will grow emotionally through communication with him or her. There is no external criterion that can either guarantee the presence of emotional resources or test its presence within. The idea that a particular theoretical school is able to provide this guarantee is quite simply a fallacy born of insecurity giving rise to institutional arrogance. I am not against someone who wants to train as a psychotherapist seeking therapy; my point is that it is not a *guarantee* of emotional growth.

So let us start by imagining with an impulse of optimism a scenario where there is an encounter between a patient who is impoverished emotionally and a psychotherapist who has greater emotional resources: Joanna and Mrs Shuttlehen. We are going to assume that through this communication Joanna is going to grow in emotional resources. How does this come about? The image of Mrs Shuttlehen feeding Joanna from her own resources is not right. Such an image would somehow imply that Mrs Shuttlehen's resources would diminish—but we believe that this is not how it works. My own experience tells me that when I have been in the psychotherapist's chair in such a situation, rather than experiencing a diminishing of my own resources, what occurs is, in fact, the opposite. This leads me to think that an imagery of emotional resources being like some reservoir that is full in the case of Mrs Shuttlehen but empty in the case of Joanna leads us in the wrong direction.

I think we need to think of it differently: that the full potential is there, but something has to occur to activate it. Now let us go back to Joanna and Mrs Shuttlehen. Joanna was in her early sixties and was terrified of death. These two met and talked every week. I believe in this actual instance Joanna visited Mrs Shuttlehen three times a week. When Joanna had been conversing with Mrs Shuttlehen for two years, she said one day:

"You know, I am not as afraid of death as I used to be . . ."

Mrs Shuttlehen was curious to know how this had come about, and so she said,

"I wonder how that change has come about?"

and Joanna replied,

"Well, Agnes, I believe *you* have been able to face death, and the fact that you have been has freed me to do so also."

Now I want to take Joanna's reply and take it provisionally as a truth and see what it tells us. What she says is that if Agnes is able to face death, then this enables Joanna to face it also. This for me is a very striking statement; let us try to draw out its implications.

First I want to generalize the statement about Joanna's fear of death in two directions—away from Joanna in particular, to all people. Therefore:

If in an engaged relationship between two people one of the two has faced her fear of death, then the other person has a good chance of being able to do so also.

And then to generalize it as to subject matter to include more than the fear of death:

* *loss*: of one's mother, one's child, one's lover, one's own illusions, one's youth, a friendship, one's family of origin, one's birthplace, one's health;
* *acceptance*: of one's mortality, one's smallness, one's limitations, one's gifts, one's abilities, one's nationality, one's prejudices, one's religious outlook, one's philosophical perspective.

The idea here is that there are facts about myself that can exist in two different states. There is a fact that is so but that I have not embraced, and there is one that I have embraced, and these two exist in me in very different ways. The next hurdle is to look at the difference between them. I quoted at the beginning that very striking statement in Paulo Coelho's novel *The Alchemist:* "Every blessing which is not accepted becomes a curse" (1974, p. 66). The idea here is that something embraced not only becomes entirely different in quality from its unembraced state but, rather, instead of enriching the personality, it becomes a corrosive poison. If this is true, then it is a psychological truth of extreme importance.

I believe that one of the most valuable contributions that Wilfred Bion made is the idea that sadness, guilt, or pain can exist in the personality without being experienced subjectively. There can be a sadness that is embraced or a sadness that exists unembraced. Bion used the term *contained*. I prefer to use the word *embrace* as it conjures up better for me the idea that it is something that I subjectively and actively do. But, for heavens sake, do not passively just imbibe this word. It fits for me, but it may not do so for you. So there is a sadness in my life and I *embrace* it, or there is a sadness that I do not *embrace*. The word *embrace* suggests something that I put my arms around. I hold it within the membrane of my own personality. I will give you three examples of what I mean.

I am talking to a man whose mother died when he was four years old; she died because her husband was driving at a perilous speed because he was in a furious temper with his wife. This did not come out at the beginning of the first interview, but only after two hours had passed. I noticed that nothing had been said about his mother and was about to observe that fact when he said,

"My mother was killed when I was four years old . . ."

and he spoke in a matter-of-fact way. He might have been telling me that his dishwasher had stopped working. He went on to say,

"When I mention this to friends, they look at me with shock as if I was troubled by it, but . . ."

he went on to say that his father had soon remarried, and his step-mother had looked after him . . .

"So I had no reason to be sad", he said.

He suffered, though, from sudden giddy attacks and fears of heights. He also was psychopathic in his business dealings. After a long analysis he *felt* for the first time an immense grief at the loss of his mother. At the same time he gave up his particular line of business and took up colour photography instead. The psychopathic behaviour was a hard nugget of congealed grief that had governed his slick business practices—this, slowly in the beginning but in the end suddenly, gave way to a grief that so overwhelmed him initially that he had to go into hospital for a short spell. This was a case of a change from grief unembraced to grief embraced. The act of embracing is manifest in the form of a feeling.

The second example is of a woman who had given birth to a Downs Syndrome child, and 15 years later she spoke of how the child's affection had been such a consolation to her in her life. However, relations with her husband were very bad, and her house was never dusted or cleaned. What emerged was that she had never embraced the disappointment that shook her whole system on the day that she gave birth to her daughter. A time came when she did, and she described how, when she came around from the anaesthetic required for the Caesarean section, she had first looked at her child, and as she told it she burst into tears. She spoke of this several times, each time elaborating more fully upon her feelings. A new lease of life took hold of her, and she cleaned up her house, she went on holiday with her husband for the first time in years, and she became happier. The consolations from her child's affection remained.

The third example is of an acquaintance who is a pilot with a laconic manner and dry sense of humour. He is highly intelligent but very bad-tempered. He told me once that the best philosophy to have in life is one of pessimism—because then, he told me, one is never disappointed. He said this as if recommending a medicine that would do me a great deal of good. One day he was asked to fly a charter plane to Alaska. He was going to take his wife and go on a trip once he got there. He told me of this plan in that same ironic manner. However, the plane developed engine trouble on the way. He had to land on Norfolk Island and fly back in a commercial aircraft. "Was he disappointed?" Not a bit of it—but all his mates suffered from his foul temper for at least three weeks. My conjecture is that he had not embraced the disappointment; instead, it took the form of a discharge of spleen into his mates at the aerodrome.

You might ask the question as to why there is a discharge rather than an embrace?

I believe that "discharge mode" is the consequence of a trauma—or, as I prefer to conceptualize it, the trauma in transformed mode. In other words, an original trauma, an event, exists today in a changed shape. The task for the individual thus afflicted is therefore to change the event that envelops her into a new construction within. The question of how someone is enabled to do that is our crucial question. It clearly means that the emotional resources need to grow and mature until they are able to do the work of embracing the detritus lying surrounding the personality and convert it into a new form. But can someone else in the presence of this individual trying to do this work have any influence upon the person engaged in this task? Our belief is that this other one can. The brief answer is that the other one can to the extent that he or she is a person. So I have flagged the issue—in a sense given the answer, but it requires explanation and elaboration.

First, when I *embrace* the sadness, I *feel* it. Or is it that I *know* it? I think this requires some sorting out. Knowledge is of things that I do; feelings are the registers of the sensations or stimuli that I receive. I may receive these from outside or from within my own body. Through feelings I have contact in a direct way with the experience of another. So when Evelyn is grieving for the death of her mother, I know it as a fact, but I also feel it through my own cognate experience. My mother died some years ago, and I know how I felt, and I can recall that feeling and through it I imagine myself into Evelyn's distress. But what if my mother is still alive and well? Can I imagine myself into Evelyn's sorrow? I think I can through another loss. My favourite dog died, and I was very distressed when this happened. Mrs Cassells, the teacher at my primary school whom I adored, died two years ago, and I was very distraught; so I have these experiences stored within me, and when Evelyn's mother dies, the event stirs these memories back into life, and then there is a living current between myself and Evelyn. We call this living current *sympathy*—this word is an Anglicization of the Greek. If we were to put it into real English, it would be *suffer with*. Through my own experience, either of my mother, my dog, or Mrs Cassells, I suffer with Evelyn, but this can only happen if

I have embraced my own grief at my mother's death, my dog's death, or that of Mrs Cassells.

It is possible not to embrace the fact that I shall die, not to embrace what is stirred up inside me by my mother's death, to pretend that I am impervious to my dog's death, and, after all, Mrs Cassells was elderly and her time had come. So I know what I do and feel what happens. When I embrace, I feel not the embrace but the consequences of that embrace—it is the consequence of something happening to me, but the happening can be my own act of hugging to myself what has happened. I feel not the act but, rather, the consequences of that act. When I embrace the fact of my mother's death, I feel sad. I know my own action through inference. Feelings are always the register of the object that I embrace: I feel the object, but not the action of embracing. The action I know through inference.

I want to put in an aside here about the need for all of us to work out a psychology of the emotional and mental landscape. Instincts are different from emotions; emotions are different from feelings; feelings are different from knowledge; both feelings and knowledge are different from thought. We need slowly to work out how these are different from one another and what the relation is between them, to formulate a psychology of these processes. I believe that when we speak, we need to do so with psychological accuracy. In some way psychoanalysis has been considered as a discipline separated from the mainstream investigations of psychology, so that the two neither interpenetrate nor illuminate each other.

I think this is partly because psychoanalysis is thought to be concerned with the unconscious, but this is incorrect. It is concerned with the whole mind—conscious and unconscious and the role of each and the relation between the two. Within psychiatry, the focus has been upon pathology, and therefore attention has been beamed in upon the normal. I am ignorant about what goes on in medical schools, but I turn to Antonio Damasio, who says:

> Few medical schools to this day, offer their students any formal instruction on the normal mind, instructions that can only come from a curriculum strong in general psychology, neuropsychology, and neuroscience. Medical schools do offer studies of the sick mind encountered in mental diseases, but it is indeed as-

tonishing to realize that students learn about psychopathology without ever being taught normal psychology. [1994, p. 255]

* * *

At the moment the way I am describing this sounds as if here am I in one place, and over there is that other who is separate from me and I make a bridge to link myself to him through employing my own experience plus imagination. Yet my instinct tells me that this is not right. That way of thinking is suggestive that the other is alien to me and that I make an effort to bridge the gap through reflecting on my own experience plus the aid of my imagination. The other, in this model, is essentially an object "out there" whom I then clothe with my own experience. But I do not think that is how it is. I am conscious of the other person, but we do need to realize that consciousness is not sufficient, because it always makes the realities of our environment present *as objects*. This has been emphasized by Haridas Chaudhuri in his book *The Philosophy of Love* (1987). We need something more than consciousness if our client or patient is going to solve his or her problem through communicating with us. I stress the phrase "something more" because what I have described does operate. There is an obvious truth in the fact that I am separate from this other individual who is in the room with me, and it is true that one mode of contact is precisely through communing with my own experience elaborated and expanded through imagination. But this in itself does not make contact with the reality of this other person in the room with me. If we start with the premise that here are two separate individuals, then through this procedure I am only in touch with myself. There has to be another faculty that puts me in touch with the reality of the other and myself. Now you must forgive me for going off on an excursion that may seem to some of you too abstract.

I will start with a simple vignette to be used as an analogy and no more than that. I am standing looking at a kookaburra standing on a branch of a tree some thirty yards from where I am standing. Then I hear that laughing scream, familiar to all Australians, coming from the direction of that bird. One piece of information is coming to me through my eyes and being registered in the visual cortex in the occipital lobe at the back of the brain, the other reaches me through the aural system to the cerebral cortex. But how do I join the two and come to the conclusion that the laughing screech comes from the bird I see? There is a something in me that synthesizes the two. I am only giving this as an analogy to introduce the idea that there are two independent systems. I have so far given only one: the connection to my own experiences, combined with and elaborated through imagination. However, this alone does not give me knowledge—certain knowledge—of the experiences of the other. This is, as it were, just the auditory system that records the sound of the kookaburra. How do I make direct contact with the experience of the other? I believe that one has to posit an experience of the other that is direct—that the other's experience is, in a real way, also my own experience. How does this occur? In my book *A Pattern of Madness* (Symington, 2002b) I have an opening chapter, which I entitled "Ontology"—that is, the study of reality itself. Science looks at one of the many varied forms that exist in our world. Ontology studies the reality itself rather than any one of its forms. Sometimes it is necessary to go right down to the foundations in order to solve a problem. Ontology and psychoanalysis are partners in this regard. They both probe into the root of things. G. K. Chesterton says in his book *What's Wrong with the World* that the greater the problem, the more abstract does our solution need to be. He expresses this with his characteristic wit:

> If your aeroplane has a slight indisposition, a handy man may mend it. But if it is seriously ill, it is all the more likely that some absent-minded old Professor with wild white hair will have to be dragged out of a college or laboratory to analyse the evil. The more complicated the smash, the whiter-haired and more absent-minded will be the theorist who is needed to deal with it; and in some extreme cases, no one but the man (probably insane) who invented your flying-ship could possibly say what was the matter with it. [Chesterton, 1910, p. 11]

So I resort to the "absentminded old Professor", and to solve this problem I go back to a basic reflection upon the very nature of existence itself. The only insane professor within the psychoanalytic classroom who resorted to this basic issue is Wilfred Bion. He introduced a term that he called "*O*". Now why did he call it *O*? I have heard some commentators say that they think it stands for *Origin*. I am doubtful about this, because Bion defines *O* thus: "I shall use the sign *O* to denote that which is the ultimate reality represented by terms such as ultimate reality, absolute truth, the godhead, the infinite, the thing-in-itself" (Bion, 1970, p. 26).

Bion had a habit of using Greek words to denote realities that are quite definite but difficult to describe with everyday English terms. The Greek word for reality is *Ontos*, and I believe that that is what *O* stands for. I suspect that he did not use the word *Ontos* itself but instead just *O*, because *Ontos* has been so variously interpreted and misinterpreted by contemporary philosophers.

There is one thing that I share with a frog, a stone, my next-door neighbour, or the Andromeda galaxy: existence itself. If I reflect upon it, then the mind grasps it as something not reducible to anything more simple: however rich in variety the world is, existence itself is indivisible. There is only it; there can be nothing outside it. Nothing means no-thing, no-reality, no-being. So this person sitting opposite me in my consulting-room is what I am. The deeper I reflect upon IT, the closer do I come to grasping, in a unique act of comprehension, the IT of which that person and myself are part. There is a leap from the sensuous contact with my own experience to that reality that is grasped by another faculty within me. Bion calls this faculty *intuition*, as does Chaudhuri, whom I have already mentioned: "the very essence of this is to be united with another person as a subject in a soul-to-soul union. Whatever we know intuitively is not an object, it is part of our own being" (1987, p. 32). Later he goes on: "The finite and infinite interpenetrate each other in life, the infinite dwells in the heart of the finite beings we are. And we dwell in the medium of the infinite" (p. 93).

So there are two faculties: the sensory one and the faculty of reality itself. I am not myself very happy with the term *intuition*. I started with the analogy of vision and hearing; it is very inadequate, but I wanted to point out that there are two separate faculties. How the one jumps to the other no one knows, but a great deal has been written about how this occurs. Bernard Lonergan wrote a long scholarly philosophical book on the subject, called *Insight* (Lonergan, 1957), and Arthur Koestler wrote on the same subject, though from a more psychological angle, in a book called *The Act of Creation* (Koestler, 1969). We do not know how this faculty works, but those who have studied it in detail, like Lonergan and Koestler, say that the leap from the sensory to that higher faculty occurs only after a long period of receptivity to the sensory experience stimulated by the other. Freud himself admired this capacity in Charcot, the famous neurologist who worked at the Salpetrière in Paris. Freud studied under him for four and a half months from October 1885 to February 1886. Strachey says that this period was a turning point for Freud because he changed in those few months from neuropathology to psychopathology, or from physical science to psychology. Charcot had discovered that paralyses could be brought about through hypnotic suggestion and therefore often had a psychological rather than a neurological origin. When Charcot died in 1893, Freud wrote an obituary of him; he described Charcot's method of working:

> he had the nature of an artist—he was, as he himself said, a *"visuel"*, a man who sees. Here is what he himself told us about his method of working. He used to look again and again at the things he did not understand, to deepen his impression of them day by day, till suddenly an understanding of them dawned on him. [Freud, 1893f, p. 12]

"Suddenly an understanding of them dawned on him." We cannot explain this leap any more than we can explain quite how Archimedes suddenly realized that he could solve the problem that Hieron of Syracuse had placed him with. Hieron had been given a crown that was purported to be made of gold—but was it? Archimedes knew the specific weight of gold, but how was he to know whether this crown, with all its delicate filigree work, was pure gold without melting it down? Then suddenly, as he was letting himself into the baths of Syracuse and water flowed out of the bath as his body lowered into it, he saw in a flash that he could weigh the crown, put it into water, and measure the amount of water it displaced. He could then put the same weight of gold and see whether it displaced the same amount. If the crown displaced more, then there was also a base metal mixed with the gold in the crown. So excited was Archimedes that it is said that he ran through the streets of Syracuse shouting "Eureka, Eureka". Quite how he moved from the observation of sensory qualities to that abstraction which we call volume is an enigma, but all those who have studied the issue say that for it to occur, certain predisposing mental activities are needed. So the exercise of the imagination is the equivalent of Archimedes lowering himself into the bath, but it is that leap from the imaginative impression to the mental reality that remains mysterious. The problem has to be engaged with. The mind is in a state of enquiry, but all people who have written on this emphasize that this is not an anxious kind of "I must find out at all costs" but a relaxed yet determined hunt for the truth, governed by an innate curiosity—not a curiosity that is servant to a practical need, but curiosity for its own sake. It is a curiosity that goes beyond the solution of the practical task. When Archimedes ran through those ancient streets in excitement, it was not just that he had found a solution to the Tyrant Hieron's paranoid concern. He had a made a discovery about the structure of the universe that had a much wider application, and there was a thrill in that discovery—like finding a hidden treasure.

Curiosity of this particular nature, then, is one of the elements; a second element is what I would call "persistent staring" at the sensory phenomena, combined with emotional receptivity. The phenomena have to be received into the soul until that moment of transformation occurs. What is not known is how this happens, but it seems to occur after the observed phenomena have been assimilated into the mind's processing plant.

The way the above applies to the sensory phenomena we encounter is similar. The curiosity is the *sine qua non*, and the persistent staring for a long period is always necessary. The very activity of this staring is the necessary preliminary for that spark to light the transforming engine. Wilfred Bion used the metaphor of the digestive system. What certainly prevents any possibility of this happening is if, instead of being engaged in this activity, the psychoanalyst or psychotherapist is busy applying a model—whether it be Freud's theory of symptom formation, Melanie Klein's theory of part-objects, or Kohut's theory of mirroring. You simply cannot afford to waste your psychic resources in this way. You need all of what you have for the curiosity to be engaged and followed and elaborated in the persistent yet patient staring.

It is crucial, first, to realize the limited nature of our psychic resources and, second, to use these resources in any mental activity, however small it may seem. So, for instance, a patient says he knew what he was going to say before coming into the consulting-room but forgot it as soon as he walked in. There is a conundrum here, and there are several possibilities for the therapist. He might ask the patient why he forgets as soon as he enters. The patient might, if he were feeling sprightly, say that if he knew, he would not be coming for sessions at all. The point is that the therapist is using up his psychic reserves by asking the question. He is looking in the wrong place. He is searching the face of the other rather than the reservoir of his own mind. The psychotherapist requires all his psychic attention on the task of unravelling the puzzle; if he uses up his mental activity in one of the other activities, he will surely not solve the puzzle.

The underpinning of all this is the absolute character of exist-ence that penetrates—as Chaudhuri says—all the finite and limited sensory qualities. The transforming agent is existence itself, which is mind. So I want to come back to where I was a few moments ago when I said that the notion that I make contact with another through my imagination is based on the idea that this other that I am with is separate from me. I said that this is not right: there is a knowledge in the shared being and it is allowing oneself to become that, become O in Bion's formulation, that in turn allows the other to become so too. Being open to communication with O—this act of communication that is most profoundly within oneself and yet deeply in the other—that this act, which opens a channel of last-ing communication, strengthens the personality and endows it with emotional robustness that is lasting. It is that one meets this ultimate reality in an encounter with the other. This, then, is the faculty—if it is right to call it a faculty—that needs to be constantly exercised. I believe that all attention has to be turned upon it. It is a faculty that requires use and practice. Freud clearly knew this and was able to exercise it to a certain extent, but his philosophical position was not supportive of it, and therefore it never attained a central place in his clinical, technical, and theoretical practice and exposition. I believe that all trainings in psychoanalysis and psychotherapy need to put the development of this faculty centre-stage and to relegate all information about the theories of other clinicians—Klein, Kohut, Winnicott, *et alia*—into second place. A crucial element in the development of this faculty is the internali-zation of those higher principles that I mentioned in chapter 1. It is that personal act of understanding that turns me from being an agglomerate, a pretend-person, into a real person, from being a magpie to being a human. It requires a creative act to bring into being something that was already there. Just as Newton's discovery of the law of gravity was a creative act and yet produced a reality that was already there, so also does it require a creative act to bring into being principles that were already there.

What I am implying here is that the presence of a person— someone in whom these higher principles and *O* as the highest are enfleshed—is the atmosphere that is generative for the other. In some of my writings (Symington, 2002, pp. 60–61) I refer to what I have called "creative communication". This is the generative activity that flows from one person towards the other.

Now after that little excursion I want to return to Joanna, who says that she is able to face her fear of death because she feels that Agnes has been able to do so. The diversion had its purpose: what happens to a grief that I do not embrace? The idea of hugging something to myself throws up an image of someone holding something within their own territory. I see a big open parkland but around it a huge high wall, like the grounds of Blenheim Palace in Oxfordshire. But what if I don't enfold it within my own boundary fence?—Then it pours out. I have a picture of jelly in a string-bag that spills out all over the ground—you get the image. But it does not spill out over the ground; in human communication it does not happen like that. It spills out, not onto the ground, but into a series of waste-paper baskets conveniently placed all around. These waste-paper baskets are people—my mother, my wife, my brother, my sister, my father, my next-door neighbour, Mr Fielding my patient, Mrs Marillac my colleague, and even Sparkle, my pet dog. These waste-paper baskets are also my body, my sexuality— especially my sexual conduct—the future, the past, and also my manner of attaching myself to another. Now please note especially that receptacle Mr Fielding, my patient.

The picture is something like this. Here is Joanna, and she is filled with both fears of her own and the detritus from other people. And here she is now knocking at Agnes Shuttlehen's door because she is in distress. Her distress is the result of two communication failures. The first is that her fear of death was not taken into her mother's heart—the furnace that magically changes a dangerous pointed steel blade into a soft golden bird of paradise that is a delight to possess and look upon. Death, that dark thunder-cloud threatening the neighbourhood, passes by and gently waters the farmer's crops. This has not happened for Joanna. Shortly after she was born, her mother had been stricken with tuberculosis and whipped away into a sanatorium in Switzerland; Joanna was taken into the care of her father's sister, Marilyn, who was a harsh and severe woman. Joanna suffered a loss with no warm heart to succour her. So this is one reason why she has come beating upon Mrs Shuttlehen's door—yet does this quite tell us what has brought her? I imagine a narrative something like this.

All seemed well until Joanna reached the age of five and was sent off to school. On the first day her mother took her and delivered her fondly into the hands of Mrs Cassells, her teacher; but then, on the second day, her mother had arranged for a neighbour, who also had a child at the primary school, to pick Joanna up at nine in the morning. She herself left for work about ten minutes beforehand. When the neighbour arrived, Joanna hid and refused to be taken to school. She hid in a cupboard at the top of the house. All the enticements of the neighbour and the au-pair girl were fruitless. Joanna had decided that she was not going to school, and she didn't go. After five failed telephone calls, the au-pair, on the sixth, zinged through to Joanna's mother, who came home angry with wind blowing her hair to one side and making her look like an uprooted plant. As soon as she came in, Joanna ran to her and nestled into her skirt, crying copious tears. This was the picture that came into Mrs Shuttlehen's mind as Joanna began to recount her forlorn tale. Every time that a parting either occurred or threatened to occur, Joanna "created a scene", and every time she did this, people got angry with her. Her father told her she was just a clever actress; her mother said she was deliberately giving her parents trouble and pain.

I shall not go through all the events of Joanna's life as she recounted them to Mrs Shuttlehen, but a theme ran through it like a single cotton thread that joins the seam of a pair of trousers from top to bottom but is mouldy and rotten, so the seam keeps coming apart. So Joanna married, but when her husband had to go overseas on a business trip, she threw herself on the ground in a fury, and he, just like her father, said she was deliberately "creating a scene"—exactly the same words. She was so enraged that when he returned, she had moved out of the house. The marriage failed. Some years passed. Joanna visited a psychologist and had some

counselling, and then she married again. Now she is in her sixties, and death is closer than it was when she was young. She has
started to have panic attacks, and, as we have seen, she capitulates
in depression when her husband castigates her and then gets into
a rage with her younger daughter, just like her father did with
her, just like her first husband did with her, just like her present
husband does with her.

She has been seeing Mrs Shuttlehen for two years. It is now
that she made the remark that I quoted at the beginning: that she
is not as afraid of death as she was, and that she believes that this
is because Mrs Shuttlehen herself has been able to face death. Now
let us look at the different elements in this.

The first thing is quite simple: we heard Joanna telling Agnes
how she had behaved on her second day at school. Joanna had
not told this to anyone before, so the very gathering of that event
from her memory and recounting it to Agnes is itself an effective
psychological act. How? I understand it in this way. When I started
out on the lectures on which this book is based, I had some idea
of the direction in which I wanted to go. I have a compass in my
pocket and I know I want to go in a westerly direction; I know that
if I go east, I will end up in the sea, so it is to the west that I need
to go. I want to go to the Blue Mountains. Someone has told me
of a beautiful view that I can observe. I am not quite sure where
that will be, but I have a sense that I shall head towards Katoomba.
The view may not be there exactly, but perhaps if I get into that
general area, I shall find what I am looking for. Only when I see it
will I know. But as I start to recount what I know, I find that not
only I am telling you something that you did not know or had not
thought about, but in the very act of telling I grasp something that
I had not grasped before. The old adage—the best way to learn is
to teach—is completely true but why is it true?

A split second before I actually speak the words, there is a
moment when the words form in my mind. Linguists refer to this
as *verbalization*. [There is a good article on this subject, "On Verbalization", by a psychoanalyst called Charlotte Balkanyi (1964). She
says: "Speech and verbalization are not identical concepts. A frac-
tion of a second before producing speech, the speaker verbalizes
his thought. In the act of speaking the first step is verbalization,
the second is speech."] In making this formation I am doing some-

thing. I am bringing something into existence that was not there before. I gather that the impressionist artist, Claude Monet, when painting the Houses of Parliament in London, did so from a room in St. Thomas's Hospital on the opposite side of the Thames. In that room he had 200 canvases. As any painter knows, the scene changes from one second to the next, and Monet was out to try to capture each of these seconds. When he had finished, his 200 canvasses he had seen the Houses of Parliament more definitively probably than anyone had ever seen them before. This was because he actively constructed the sensations hammering on his optic nerves into a picture that had not been there before. I know, I grasp, I take in through an active constructive act. So there is one thing I know for certain: that through these lectures I have come to understand certain things that I had not understood before. I do not know whether this is true for any of you, but with regard to myself I am certain. Because I believe in a mutuality existing at the root of human intercourse, I suspect that some of you will also know something, grasp something, that you had not done so before—but, and this is important, it will not be exactly as I have delivered it to you. You, as listeners or readers, reconstruct. Charlotte Balkanyi says in that same article:

> In the listener, a reverse process, also in two steps, takes place: the first is the hearing of speech, the second is the de-verbalization of the words. Deverbalization includes non-verbal elements; the heard word sets into resonance affects and recalls memory-images. [1964, p. 64]

You will, I believe, only understand if you deverbalize, break down into your own imagery, and reconstruct it. You have a bigger job to do than I. We might turn for an analogy to the way a telephone works. When I speak into the mouthpiece, there is a diaphragm with carbon granules that is compressed and expanded according to the variations of acoustic energy that impact upon it. This converts acoustic energy into electrical impulses. At the other end of the line the process is reversed: as the electrical impulses hit the diaphragm, they re-convert into acoustic energy. In any case, this was how it was with telephones when I was at school. I suspect that the process is different now.

So coming back to Joanna, as she tells Agnes about her second day of school at the age of five, she is painting a picture out of raw sensations in the memory, so in the very act of telling she is embracing it in a way that she had not done before. You might well ask me: "Well, did Agnes have any role here? Could she have done the same without Agnes being present at all?"

This brings us back to Joanna's comment that she thought that she was not as fearful of death now because she believed that Agnes had been able to face her own death.

Let us go back to the very simple formula that I have repeated constantly: that a happening is either embraced or not embraced. If it is embraced, it is also constructed through the imaginative processes into a personal artistic product within. If it is not embraced, it remains like a foreign body within that irritates and troubles my calm. It is like a fly that keeps crawling over my face: I keep brushing it away in frustration. So, also, the happening that is not embraced is a foreign invader that I try to get rid of. I might, like Joanna, try get rid of it by shouting at my younger daughter or by letting my spouse castigate me, or I might go on a drinking bout or throw myself into work in impassioned intensity or be in a cycle where all of these occur. Or I discharge it into my body, and I develop an ulcer in my colon or rape a young child or arrange for someone to whip me in a sexual orgy and . . . the possibilities are numerous, but the underlying principle is an activity the purpose of which is to discharge a foreign body, an event that has not been embraced.

So, looked at in this light, we could say that Joanna's formulation is that when she senses that Mrs Shuttlehen is able to embrace the fact of her own death, then she, Joanna, is also able to do this. In other words, what would prevent Joanna from doing so is if Agnes cannot embrace the fact of her death. Let us, for a moment, suppose an alternative coupling: the psychotherapist, George Underhill, has not embraced the fact of his death, and Joanna is seeing him rather than Agnes. George is discharging, and this prevents Joanna from embracing her own death. For her to be able to embrace it she needs the other person to be able to do so. The psychotherapist's capacity to embrace painful events is the precondition for the patient to be able to do so also. There is nothing I can do to *make* someone else freely embrace—that is an act that occurs within. Only Joanna can generate that. It has to be out of her own freedom. The recognition of that is itself important. In fact, if I impose, even ever so slightly, upon the other, then I am discharging, and I create conditions that make the inner act of embracing, if not impossible, at least extremely difficult.

In chapter 5 I trace through the interpretations that Agnes made to Joanna, but keeping this underlying principle in mind.

CHAPTER FIVE

Communication and representation

The question: *How is it that someone who has a problem is able to resolve it through conversation with another?*

". . . our operations, our very intentions, will be moulded in some way on the object they tend toward in order to receive their form there."

Maurice Blondel [1984, p. 207]

W e reached an important point in chapter 4. There is a gap between the sensuous imagery that we form out of the sensations that come into us and the mental concept through which this abundant imagery is captured and unified into a single unbodily relational reality. I say "relational" to pick up the point made in chapter 2, where I quoted the Canadian philosopher, Peter March, as defining mind as the relation between two objects, which harmonized with Charles Birch's notion of mind-stuff existing in the relation between subatomic particles. It is real, though not material—it is in the space-between. So what we came to was that somehow someone jumps across that gap from the sensuous to the unbodily representation. The classic example of this is

Archimedes, who had been given the task of discovering whether or not King Hieron's crown was of pure gold, but the same applies when a psychoanalyst or psychotherapist is listening to a mass of detailed description from a patient and suddenly an act of comprehension unifies all this detail into an unbodily element. But it is precisely this unifying act of comprehension that "solves a problem". This is linked to what I said in chapter 1: that it is the placing of an alienated element in relation to others through the agency of a *common denominator* that loosens the problem, and light flows in where there had been darkness before. But we are still left with the question of how one gets from one to the other. What is it that pushes me over that gap? And here I have to make a diversion because the very word "push" is rooted in the instinct theory that most of us in this field have been reared upon. It is a very good example of the way in which a theory, a background theory, can blind us to something that is in front of our eyes.

When I give an interpretation that "clicks" for the patient, what is happening? The word "click" means that there is a spontaneous inner assent. There is often something that resists assenting—it may be a blow to one's self-esteem, or the positions that one has espoused, or one's public image, it may be a humiliation. Often there is a struggle, but let us say that in this struggle I go with the invitation to assent. Now note that I use the word "invitation". I am not forced to assent. The very word "assent" means that it is something freely given from within. An interpretation is an understanding given by the analyst to the patient, but its effectiveness depends upon whether or not there is inner assent. (Inner assent is not always immediately manifest: I can think of a patient who said to me, *"I did think you were right, but I wouldn't have dreamt of telling you that at the time"*—and so on.) Of course, an analyst or psychotherapist can persuade a patient to agree to something; the power of persuasion can be very great, with the result that the patient submits outwardly but grinds his or her teeth inwardly. The danger of such submission is particularly great in those who train and want to qualify. A colleague told me that she submitted to interpretations that she knew were not correct because she wanted to qualify and not be stopped from doing so. As soon as she qualified, she terminated her analysis. When in the years between 1892 and 1896 Freud made the move from treating with hypnotism to treating with what he came to call "psychoanalysis", he was moving from *persuasion* to *invitation*. Of course, by no means did he succeed entirely, as his altercations with colleagues like Jung and Adler demonstrate only too clearly, but the philosophical intent behind that move from hypnotism to psychoanalysis was one from a desire to *dominate* to a desire to *emancipate*. There is, of course, much hypnotic persuasion within psychoanalysis and within psychotherapy. I mention this to distinguish it from interpretation and its response, which is assent, not submission.

Assent is freely given. I cannot be pushed into assent. If I am pushed, then it is not assent. I have no doubt at all that there is an *inviting presence* in the personality. I shall try to give instances of this.

A friend rings me because he has been falsely accused of a criminal act. Could I come to court on the following Friday and give a character witness? I say, "No, I am sorry, I just cannot make it on Friday—I have a full work schedule that day", but later my response troubles me. I remember that he had helped me some years earlier, and he is an old friend. I do not want to go all the way to Canberra on a Friday, to cancel my patients, and so on, but something inside beckons me to go. I think about it, and I decide to go—and as soon as I have done so I know that what I have decided is right.

A man, Donald Jarrett, is deriving benefit from his therapy with Mrs Shuttlehen. Why did he not come to her four years earlier? All is useless. He will give up. Mrs Shuttlehen points out that he is saying this because he is deriving benefit from the therapy, and he only wishes that he had come four years earlier because then he might not have become so disastrously involved with Anita. So he is experiencing a good thing, says Mrs Shuttlehen, but his regret at not having come sooner is now covering the good thing. Now that is a truth. The interpretation is a statement of how things are operating inside him. It does not tell him that he should be glad that he is having therapy now or that he should be grateful for what he has got: it is purely a statement of what seems to be happening within. Now something beckons Donald to look at the inner scene that has just been drawn, something invites him to let the good thing have the focus of his attention—just as I rethought things and decided to go to the court in Canberra for my friend. If Mrs Shuttlehen had instead said that instead of moaning he should be grateful for the therapy he is receiving now, then she would have blinded his eyes to the inner scene, and the *inviting presence* within would not have had a chance to come into operation. Donald has not been given an interpretation but has been subtly bullied.

Now my theoretical aside is this. We all have in us a thrust to survive, and this thrust is instinctual. The instincts, often called drives in psychoanalytic discourse, are there despite ourselves. I can, it is true, through the agency of my omnipotence, pretend that I am not hungry or not thirsty or that when someone burns me with a match it does not hurt. I have in me the power to mobilize forces that anaesthetize the instincts, but such power is always temporary, always a transient condition. I am driven by thirst, by hunger, by cold, by heat, by pain. I am not a free agent. I am the slave of survival. Survival needs impel me. My own individuality is servant to a biological purpose: the propagation of the species of which I am an insignificant member. Now it is precisely this theory that rules like a victorious empress over the social sciences, which very easily blinds us to the reality that free assent is *the* response to an interpretation. Survival does not have any knowledge of such a thing as free assent. When our ancestors of 30,000 years ago started to paint as they did in the caves in southern Europe, they took hold of instruments fit for survival needs and used them as ends in themselves. My intention in chapter 2 was to lay down this principle upon which civilization has since then been based—that this ancient mutation enters into the very fabric of our relations with one another here today. So my aside is to draw your attention to what is commonly called "instinct theory" and give place instead to one that recognizes an *inviting presence* within the personality.

Returning now to the gap between the sensuous and the emotional understanding, there is in me an invitation to jump over that gap. It may be that King Hieron would have had Archimedes beheaded if he had not solved his problem, and it was this that pushed our ancient inventor into the momentous discovery. The *invitation* is rarely pure and simple, but, as I said in chapter 4, when Archimedes ran through the streets of Syracuse shouting "Eureka!", it was not only because he had satisfied his paranoid employer, but for the sheer of joy of a scientific discovery. It is very rare that a motive is pure. My sorting survival instincts to one side and action prompted by free inner invitation to the other is not to claim that it is always one or the other but to highlight that free inner invitation is a distinct motivational principle, both within the individual and within civilization, even though it is only rarely found unwedded to the instincts for survival. It is always the complexity of human beings and the principles that guide them in their endeavours that social scientists attempt to tailor to our limited minds, those restricted inner laboratories, so that what is multiform is pounded ruthlessly into something single and uniform.

Here, then, is this gap that the patient is standing in front of, and hopefully the psychoanalyst or psychotherapist is not standing there with a whip forcing him or her to leap over it. What is it that the therapist has to do? Briefly, she has to become an *embodied invitation*. Let us try to see what this means.

The *inner inviting presence* has to be reflected in the person of the psychoanalyst or psychotherapist. Even that is not right: rather, a person is the free response to the *inner inviting presence*, and the alternative is an *aggregate* mode of being. I was asked how I could tell whether someone's statement that he had not been able to commit himself was just being said to please or was the expression of an inner realization. Another way of putting that would have been to ask whether that patient was in *aggregate* or *unified* mode. The point I am getting at here is that *unification* takes place when the different parts of the personality are carried forth as one in the wake of a free response to the *inner inviting presence*. So when we ask whether it is *genuine* or *fake,* we mean is it external accommodation where the individual is in *aggregate* mode, or are we witnessing inner free assent? If it is the former, we refer to it being *fake*; if the latter, we call it *genuine*. And, further, we have in us a faculty that is able to differentiate, and this faculty is not that which processes the sense data but one that penetrates behind the words to the composition of the inner being: it is able to differentiate between a unified presence and one that is an *aggregate*. We do truly have an X-ray faculty. The problem is that it is very easily obscured. The therapist can either increase this obscurity or, on the other hand, make it more evident, so it becomes effective within the personality.

The psychotherapist's task, then, is to be the embodiment of this *inner inviting presence*. I have quite often come across situations like this. A therapist makes what he believes to be a transference interpretation. I say to him, "Is that what you thought?" and the answer comes back that it was not truly what he thought but what he believed he *ought* to say. He is in *fake* mode rather than in genuine identity with who he is. He has not responded to the *inner inviting presence* but has instead been carried like a bundle of ill-assorted junk by an alien body that is inhabiting his mortal frame. He is being invited to embrace his own thought, and something is preventing it. In this case it is a recommendation that therapists in the psychodynamic school should make a transference interpretation, and this dictum is interfering with what *he* truly thinks. It is not that there is anything wrong with a transference interpretation, but it is being conceptualized at the lower-order level instead of the higher-order level. At the higher-order level it would not exert any pressure upon the psychotherapist, whereas on the lower level—the sensuous processing level—it does.

The situation, then, is that there is the patient, and within her is this *inner inviting presence,* but it is overlaid by a counterforce, which Helen Garner, in her essay, "Killing Daniel", calls a force-field (1996, p. 167), by which she means a hypnotic power that grips a whole group and holds it paralysed. It is this power that takes hold of a group but also takes hold of and smothers the inner spirit of the individual.

We are familiar with what I am talking about in a different language form. We call this *force-field* a psychosis where chaotic elements are projected. Where projection is happening, there is psychosis. To the extent that I am overwhelmed by this, to this very extent am I also in a psychotic state. It is here that language is deceiving because truly in this state there is no *"I"*. It is inner unification that constitutes what we call *I,* whereas when *I* is constituted by a bundle of bits, carried like dust before the wind, the word *I* is a lie. This is why I draw a distinction between an individual and a person. An individual is a bundle of bits held together by a membrane made of omnipotence but which is inwardly subject to the outer *force-field,* whereas a person is an inwardly created unified presence. A person neither projects elements outward nor can be projected into. I hear from time to time psychoanalysts or psychotherapists saying that they are being projected into. This means that they are in *aggregate* mode. In this mode, an individual feels deeply shamed—of no worth. I refer to this in my book *A Pattern of Madness* (Symington, 2002b) as a *worm*. There is an inner knowledge that there is the possibility of being differently constituted.

Of course we are not persons full stop. We are constantly being called to be persons. I think I am a person, but then meet someone—perhaps a patient, perhaps my next-door neighbour, perhaps a work-mate—and I am blown hither and thither and I know I am in *aggregate* mode, so my task is to start a work inside myself. It is the work of transforming this chaos into personhood. The *inner inviting presence* is to be master of the world and not this alien force pounding and invading the inner perimeter.

The paradox, however, is this: the extent to which I am able to be a person gives the other inhabitant of my consulting-room the opportunity of being so also. This is, I believe, because I then embody my own *inner inviting presence,* and this has a generative effect upon the other. This faculty that I have been referring to passes beyond the sense of the outer words to the inner constituting mode of the other. If I am a person, it does not mean that I force the other into the way in which I am constituted. This is what I do when I am in *aggregate* mode—or, more accurately, this is what the *force-field* contained in this individual claiming falsely to be an *I* forces itself upon the other. A person is fulfilled by the presence of another person, so there is an inherent need for the other to be different. If I, as psychoanalyst or psychotherapist, embody my own *inner inviting presence,* then it has a strengthening effect upon the *inner inviting presence* of the other. If this were not the case, then the patient would be just as well if she stayed at home and read a book.

We are not just mental beings but *embodied spirits,* and now is the moment to consider the body that until now has been ignored.

We said in chapter 1 that meaning seemed to come about through a theoretical *common denominator* linking up a series of discrete elements, and meaning *is* the unity underlying the diversity. This *common denominator* is, however, made up of a series of representations, not just of one. What I see, what I hear, what I feel are all inner representations of stimuli hitting the organism either from the outside world or from within the organism, the latter being known as the *proprioceptive and interoceptive senses* (*interoception* is of the viscera; *proprioception* is of the muscles and joints). These representations are constructed images. As Damasio says:

> the images we experience are brain constructions *prompted* by an object, rather than the mirror reflections of the object. . . . There is no picture of the object being transferred optically from the retina to the visual cortex. The optics stop at the retina. Beyond that there are physical transformations that occur in continuity from the retina to the cerebral cortex . . . There is a set of *correspondences* which has been achieved in the long history of evolution, between the physical characteristics of objects independent of us and the menu of possible responses of the organism. [Damasio, 2003, p. 200]

As representation that is a particular mental image is central to the thinking here, I want to try to elucidate as far as I am able the mechanics of this process. So far I have said nothing about the recent findings of neuroscience. The main reason is my own ignorance, but there is another. I have tried to designate here what is central and to distinguish between what is primary and what is secondary. Neuroscience and its elaboration is in the secondary department, and I sense a danger of it being made primary. Also, we are looking for an understanding of how it is that a person with a problem can resolve it through communication with another, and clearly an obvious point must be that the presence of the other must have some effect upon the patient or client. This truth is very likely to be a particular instance of a more general principle: that the human being is affected by the encounter with the bit of the world in which he or she is located. I shall try here to make a résumé of the neurobiological underpinnings of this principle. I want you to know, however, that this is not well integrated thinking on my part. I am sitting at the feet of Antonio Damasio, my mentor, and distilling what he has told me in his three books—*Descartes' Error* (1994), *The Feeling of What Happens* (2000), and *Looking for Spinoza* (2003)—and to a lesser extent what I have learned from Susan Greenfield's book on the human brain (2003). Damasio is a wonderful teacher: he has the gift of being able to explain complicated matters in clear language and imagery, and this even to someone who has not studied biology or anatomy at advanced level. So here goes.

I am standing on a mountain path looking at a beautiful wide river, and as I do so, I hear the familiar honking of geese flying overhead; at the same time I smell the sweet fragrance of some wild lavender that is growing close to where I am standing. I am not very comfortable, though, because a stone has got into my shoe, and there is a biting pain in the sole of my right foot. I am eating a cherry, which I picked off a tree that I had just passed. So how do I manage to see the river, hear the geese, smell the lavender, register the pain in my foot, and taste the flavour of this succulent cherry? The simplest picture I can give you is of a Plasticine substance that moulds itself to the shapes of the stimuli that bombard it. Imagine a large lump of Plasticine and a sculptor or potter hitting it here, banging it there, so its shape is inevitably changed by these energetic movements of pushing, pulling and thumping that are being rained upon it. Something like this is happening as I stand upon my mountain path looking at the river. Varying shades of light and colour shaped to a certain form bombard the rods, cones, and retina of the eye. The sound waves from the geese overhead hit the cochlea of my ears, minute fragments of lavender touch my olfactory nerves in my nose, the peripheral nerve endings in the skin of my foot are being assaulted by the stone in my shoe, and the juice of the cherry has impacted upon the taste buds at the back of my tongue. The Plasticine is being shaped by the hammering of nature's sculptor that totally surrounds me. The *proprioceptive* and *interoceptive senses* map all these stimuli in the brain.

The sensations that I experience result from the changes in my body's shape. Seeing, hearing, smelling, tasting, and touching are all registrations of the sculptor's active hitting of this sensitive lump of matter. Analogies always break down: the defect of this one is that Plasticine is dead matter, but what we are looking at is a living organism, so it does not deliver itself up as a passive victim to the blows that rain upon it. The organism engages actively with the environmental sculptor. The sculptor analogy has, however, a certain aptness even in this respect. The sculptor is conditioned by his material. A block of marble resists him in one way, clay in another, Plasticine in another, and so on. Maurice Blondel, whom we have already quoted, says:

> some matter, whatever it may be, is indispensable for the exercise of our activity as a prior condition—but also our

operations, our very intentions will be moulded in some way on the object they tend toward in order to receive their form there. [1984, p. 207]

This clearly has a link with what I said in chapter 2, where, quoting Charles Birch the biologist, I said that the relationship to the other—the other element—has even an *internal* effect on the one and the other. So what we refer to as the "sensations" are nature's sculpting blows that alter the shape of the organism. Although these things are happening to me at different sites of the organism, yet there is a unity. There are organizing principles. We need now, then, to move to another analogy that I take from Damasio. There is a head that is the site of the *central nervous system,* and there is a body into which flows a mass of tributaries from the central nervous system known as the *peripheral nervous system.* The nerves or neurons are a complex system of communication within the organism. The light rays from the river hit the retina of my eye, but these are transformed in the neuronal pathway from the retina to the visual cortex, which is located in the occipital lobe at the back of my head. There is a similar story with the sound waves that hit the cochlea of my ear, the minute particles of lavender that hit the olfactory nerves, the cherry juice that touches my taste buds, and, finally, the nerves in my foot, which are being rudely assaulted by the obstructive shape of the stone in my shoe.

What we are saying, then, is that different body parts—the eye, the ear, the nose, the tongue, and the skin—are affected, and each of these changes at the outer circumference of the body is conveyed along pathways to the brain. A signal like an electrical impulse travels from the nerve cell down its *axon* and over to the *dendrite* of another cell. The *axon* is a fibre going out from the cell, whereas the *dendrite* is fibre that carries an impulse into the cell. Between cells, or groups of cells, there is a gap known as a *synapse.* On arrival at the *synapse,* the electrical impulse sets off a chemical that crosses the gap. This chemical is known as a *neurotransmitter,* and it carries the message across the gap but in a more distributed fashion than the electrical impulse. So messages come from the body to the brain, and the brain also sends messages back to the various body sites. There is some coordinating centre in the brain that forms a *neural map* or a *neural pattern.*

The inner neurological system is in the service of communication. It is the physical communication structure. Damasio has shown how an emotional stimulus, or what he refers to as an ECS—an *emotionally competent stimulus*—is registered in the brain before the individual is subjectively aware of this. Paul Whalen, a researcher, showed stimuli very rapidly to normal people who were unaware of what they were seeing: brain scans revealed that nevertheless the amygdala became active (Damasio, 2003, p. 60). In another experiment researchers were studying brain activity that corresponded with the feelings of happiness, sadness, fear, or anger; here, again, they found that changes in skin conductivity always preceded the signal that a feeling was being felt. Electrical monitors registered the seismic activity of emotion unequivocally before the feeling was registered (pp. 100–101). This validates Damasio's view that emotional states come first, and feelings follow. It also confirms my view that the emotion is the communicative action and the feelings are the radar screen that picks them up. I believe that this distinction between emotions and feelings is crucial for our understanding in our work as psychotherapists.

Damasio is referring here to dispositional neural patterns that are physically constructed; he calls them "neural maps" or "neural patterns". When I talk of representations, I am referring to the subjective correlate of these. No one has yet come up with an answer to how it is that we get from the dispositional neural patterns to the subjective representation. Damasio himself is clear that

> There is a major gap in our current understanding of how neural patterns become mental images. . . . Most consciousness studies are actually centered on this issue of the making of the mind, the part of the consciousness puzzle that consists of having the brain make images that are synchronized and edited into what I have called the "movie-in-the-brain". But these studies do not provide an answer to the puzzle yet, and I wish to make it clear that I am not providing an answer either. [2003, p. 198]

You will notice that there are gaps right up the information pathway. We do not know how the leap occurs between the neural patterns and the mental images; we do not know how we get from the sensations to the concept, as I tried to illustrate in chapter 4 with the example of Archimedes. Also in the details of the thinking process there is a leap from the sensation-image to a thought. We do not know how these gaps are traversed. It is also, I believe, a mistake to assume automatically that the neural map fashions the mental image. That the two are interrelated is almost certain, but that the former causes the latter is an assumption—one that has, I know, gone almost unchallenged in the scientific community but . . . very great minds in the past have thought that it is the other way round: that mind creates nature and not the other way around. This question will have to be left on one side. I support the view of Charles Birch and the *panexperientialists* who believe that mind and brain are two aspects of one thing. I follow Kant in believing that our minds are not able to grasp certain antinomies—they are too limited. What I want to address now is how it is that communication fashions an inner representation. Just in case you think that this is entirely an idiosyncratic idea of my own, I would draw your attention to the fact that Wilfred Bion's idea of the mother's *reverie* functioning as an agent for the infant's internal psychic organization implies that the external communicative mode leaves a lasting imprint upon the infant's psychological makeup. So what we need to inquire into is how the communication with another ends up with the creation of an inner representation.

I want to emphasize that the whole neurological setup is a communication network. To think of bodily changes just as one of our communicative modes is of great help in unifying mind and body under the hegemony of one guiding principle.

The reception of the other's communication inside myself must somehow hold the key. We already know that the reception of sense data is transformed within into representations. What we are claiming here is that this is also the case with human communication. Damasio refers to "brain constructions"; representations are the subjective correlate of these. Communication with another human being requires more, however, than just receptivity to sensations. I have to do something in order to understand what the other is trying to communicate to me. The other already has a theoretical construction of understanding, although it may not be properly articulated. Everyone has a theory within them that is used to explain the phenomena that he encounters both within himself and outside himself. Very often the theory is inadequate.

I will give an example that is currently quite relevant. Someone believes that goodness is entirely a subjective personal idea. This implies that there is no possibility of ever reaching a reality outside myself—I am the judge of all that there is: there is no outside agent who could come and tap me on the shoulder and say: "But have you ever thought of this. . . ." Yet representation implies some third element within the personality. Let me elaborate on this. I need to come to it in two different ways.

The first is the way in which what is communicated to the external person represents what is understood within. I will start with two examples. A woman always spoke of her father in very derogatory terms: that he used to insult her, call her a whore, that she would be better living in the madhouse than at home. Nothing good was ever spoken of him by her. Then one day she mentioned that he loved birds, and when she was young, he used to take her to watch a kingfisher by the river near their home. Now in the early period of my psychoanalytic career I would have said,

"You have never told me this before . . ."

and I would imply that this had been consciously withheld until now. This, of course, carries a reproachful message:

"You should have told me long ago. Go to your desk and write out an apology and promise me that you will never do that again . . ."

In a moment of good fortune I gave this Headmaster Neville the sack. I dismissed him from my consulting-room. My patients breathed a sigh of relief. I understood that this woman had not told me because she had not realized until then that her father loved birds and that he enjoyed her company and teaching her to love looking at the kingfisher by the river close to their home. I understood that the moment when she communicated this piece of information to me coincided with her own inner realization of her father's love of nature and his gentleness towards herself. So there was a correlation between the inner realization and the communication to me. In some way these two entities were two sides of one coin—the moment of communication symbolized the inner realization. Would it be right to say that one caused the other? I believe not. I think the two are the product of an activity that is going on at a deeper level, they are manifestations of an unseen but deeper activity. But what is this?

I think this relates to a subject already brought up in chapter 2 on emotions. One of the points I made there is that the emotion itself is *associated* with physical states, but in itself it is an invisible or non-sensuous activity. I will quote this passage from William James:

> I now proceed to urge the vital point of my whole theory, which is this: If we fancy some strong emotion and then try to abstract from our consciousness of it all the feelings of its bodily symptoms, we find we have nothing left behind, no "mind-stuff" out of which the emotion can be constituted, and that a cold and neutral state of intellectual perception is all that remains. [1989, p. 744]

This theory of William James's, which Damasio supports and believes, was prophetical in that it was years ahead of its time. It chimes with my own view that emotion itself is not detectable. However, I disagree with James's view that it is therefore *"a cold and neutral state of intellectual perception"*. There is no reason why it should be "cold"—this is not a neutral statement. After all, why not call it "hot"? I think we understand what he means, though. Anger that is reflectively embraced can be present in the personality in a calm state. For instance, it may have become an anger that has the quality of silent determination. In such a state it will be an anger that is effective rather than impotent. Someone in a stirred-up state of rage, with flailing arms and nostrils that inflate and dilate with heavy breathing, is frequently impotent and only laughed at or patronized by those around him. However, I think that William James's observation can be interpreted differently—namely, that the "nothing left" that he talks about is the emotion that has no sensation qualities, and this is certainly the view that Bion took of it. James said that because it had no sensation qualities, therefore it did not exist. Bion interpreted that differently by saying that it does exist, but it has no sense qualities attached to it.

We have to start probing hither and thither to try to come up with an answer—at least a tentative answer—to what it is that underlies both the communication to the other and the inner psychic realization. I think that both inner realization and communication are the products of an inner creative activity. If you ask me to prove this, I find it difficult; the best I can do is to point to facts that support this viewpoint. John Henry Newman said that some social facts are proved through a *convergence of probabilities*. I think the proof that we are looking for is something of this kind. The first fact I go back to is to look at the caves at Lascaux and Altamira where our primitive ancestors painted the bison and other animals on the ceilings of those ancient caves. I had the good fortune as an adolescent to visit Altamira and see those paintings. Today tourists who are not palaeontologists are not allowed into the cave; instead, they have to visit a modern replica close to the site. The paintings in these two caves are the first evidence of human creative endeavours; they indicate the artist's ability to detach a piece of landscape in his mind and transfer it onto the ceiling of the cave. There is a capacity here to select something particular from the landscape—a bison, in this case—and represent it on the cave ceiling. Of course, in its actual physical properties this representation has very little in common with the beast charging around on the plain: it is many times smaller, it has no fur, it does not move, it smells quite different, it is only partially three-dimensional. The painting is something created out of these materials in order to represent the beast in the field. It is something that a person has created, and he relies on his viewers to have inside them the same structures that will enable them to recognize from those few sparse lines and colour the beast in the field that he is trying to portray. It seems as if there must be within the human organism a certain set of lines, curves, and colours sufficient to represent the huge variety of forms that we encounter in the world around us. Creation, then, is a refashioning of these inward forms accurately enough to measure up to the sensational patterns that we perceive in the world around us. A representation is always a creation. It seems that perception is the assemblage of elements within, so that they correspond to what exists outside the organism. Damasio says: "There is a set of *correspondences* which has been achieved in the long history of evolution, between the physical characteristics of objects independent of us and the menu of possible responses of the organism" (2003, p. 200). This seems to mean, then, that the materials, as it were, for representing the outer world are present in the neural resources of our brains. There seems also to be evidence for this from neuroscience. Damasio goes on: "the images we experience are brain constructions *prompted* by an object, rather than the mirror reflection of the object" (2003, p. 200). To prove this, Damasio quotes from the studies of David Hubel and Torsten Wiesel: "They showed that an experimental animal (a monkey) looking at a straight line, curved line, or lines positioned at varied angles will form distinct patterns of neural activity in its visual cortex" (Hubel, 1988).

Here, then, are two probabilities that seem to converge towards the same conclusion: that a representation is something created. Is there a third probability? I fall back here on the two theories of Kant and of Bion.

I am neither competent nor able to detail Kant's theory of knowledge, but the aspect of it that is relevant to this discussion is his view that it is *a priori* judgements that unify the sensations coming into us from the outside world. *A priori* judgements are those that are made out of what is in the mind, outside space and time. It is, then, the same idea as that put forward by Damasio: that there are forms in the mind that have a correspondence to the way the external world is. The difference between Kant and Damasio here is that for Kant the *a priori* is a feature of the mind, whereas for Damasio it is a feature of the brain. There are elements in the mind, according to Kant, or brain, according to Damasio, that are capable of construction into a form that synthesizes and corresponds to the world of sensation. It is not, of course, a proof to say that Kant saw things in a way that is consistent with what I am proposing. You have every right to say that this is purely the argument from authority, and I cannot gainsay this. One of the reasons why Kant's philosophy had such a groundbreaking impact upon Western thought was that it brought together romantic subjectivity with scientific objectivity and showed how the two could be brought together. When a particular form of thinking has such an impact, we might stop to ponder whether it did not select for attention a particular feature that had been either ignored or dismissed until then.

Bion also had a constructivist view of the mind. He believed that there was a fundamental constructing principle in the personality, which he called "alpha function". Maurice Blondel, whom I have quoted several times, had a similar view:

> therefore the synthesis is something more than the immense multitude of its conditions, there has to be in it something to contain and dominate this very immensity; a remainder that no doubt is as little as nothing and which the sciences take into account only to eliminate it; but it is this nothing which, from an interior viewpoint, is everything, since it is the invisible principle of the synthesis, the soul of all positive knowledge and of every efficacious operation. [1984, p. 98]

He continues:

> the subjective is precisely that which cannot be known either in function of mathematics or in function of sensible observation, because it is that which constitutes their bond and introduces unity amid multiplicity. [pp. 103–104]

This view of Blondel and of Bion is not the majority view, and those who want to understand Bion will have in their minds to disengage his thought from the background that is probably more familiar. It was through this agency working at a deep level in the personality that disorganized sensations are moulded into a pattern. I believe that Bion came upon this formulation through treating psychotic patients: that the flaw in psychotic patients was that this creative principle had been either stifled or prevented from coming into being, and that Blondel, on the other hand, came to his through being deeply rooted in the philosophy of Aristotle and of the mediaeval Scholastic philosophers. However, when he came to write his thesis on Action in the last decade of the nineteenth century in Paris, his colleagues thought he was batty. It is interesting that when Damasio started looking at the neurobiology of feelings, he met with similar disdain, as he mentions at the beginning of *Looking for Spinoza*:

> When I started musing about how the brain managed to create the mind, I accepted the established advice that feelings were out of the scientific picture. . . . It took me awhile to see the degree to which the injunction was unjustified and to realize that the neurobiology of feelings was no less viable than the neurobiology of vision or memory. [2003, pp. 4–5]

It is interesting, though, that Bion, through the treatment of psychotic patients, arrived at a psychological view that was a very ancient one and one that had been almost entirely repudiated in modern times. To understand what is the creative force that underlies the communication and the fashioning of an inner representation, we have to free ourselves, I believe, from the dominant scientific paradigm.

Bion, then, designed a developmental structure the foundation of which was a series of diffuse chaotic sensations that were gathered into creative coherence by the agency he called "alpha function" (Bion, 1962/84, p. 25). Madness occurs when this agency is paralysed. His theory aimed to explain sane mental life, but it arose out of his observation of those who are mad and was therefore an attempt to explain what had gone astray in the mad mind. He had noted that psychotic patients rarely dreamt, and he saw dreaming as the early synthetic personal activity that is the artistic work of an inner creator: "alpha function". Bion's view of dreaming was quite different from Freud's theory: whereas for Freud the dream was the expression of a culturally prohibited wish-fulfilment, for Bion it was the manifestation of an inner creative and synthesizing process.

Given the concurrence of Bion's views with those of Kant, it is not surprising that the former recommended the reading of Kant to candidates in the institutes of psychoanalysis in Brazil when he visited there a few times in his final years.

I shall say here in an aside that in order to understand the psychology of the inner world—and the outer too, for that matter—we need to stretch our curriculum to include a number of thinkers who are at the present time not included in programmes of study for candidates in psychoanalytic institutes. I want now to consider one such thinker.

I am referring to John Henry Newman, an Anglican Divine who, having been born in 1801, straddled almost the whole of the nineteenth century, dying at the age of 90 in the last decade of the century. He, together with Pusey and Keble, was the leader of the Oxford Movement, which flourished in the first half of the nineteenth century, the ecclesiastical goal of which was the restoration of sacramental life in the Anglican Church. However, they

had a deeper cultural purpose: to revolt against the liberal utilitarian spirit of the time. Newman converted to Roman Catholicism
in 1845. Much later he was made a Cardinal, and he lived out his
clerical life at Edgbaston, near Birmingham. He was one of the
great scholars of the nineteenth century; he is said to have studied
for 14 hours every day, and his collected letters run to about 20,000
in number, many of them long dissertations on matters philosophical, theological, and historical. He may be familiar to some as the
author of the Anglican hymn *Lead Kindly Light,* which he wrote in
1833, and much later, in 1865, of the poem *The Dream of Gerontius,*
which was in 1900 turned into a musical oratorio by Elgar. When
he was Chancellor of Dublin University, Newman gave the eight
lectures that were later published as *Idea of a University* (1927); this,
to my mind, is the greatest treatise on education ever written. In
1870 he published *A Grammar of Assent,* a philosophical work the
aim of which was to establish the emotional roots of certainty. He
coined the phrase "the illative sense", by which he meant the primary elements of thinking that lay in a hidden personal orientation
to the world and governed the way a thinker assembled his facts,
selected some and left out others, and gave them an interpretative
schema. Taking five authorities on the state of Greece and Rome
in their classical period—Niebuhr, Clinton, George Lewis, Grote,
and Colonel Mure—Newman showed that they all had access to
the same facts:

> These authors have severally views of their own on the period
> of history which they have selected for investigation, and they
> are too learned and logical not to know and to use to the utmost
> the testimonies by which the facts which they investigate are
> to be ascertained. Why then do they differ so much from each
> other, whether in their estimate of those testimonies or of those
> facts? because that estimate is simply their own, coming of their
> own judgment; and that judgment coming of assumptions of
> their own, explicit or implicit; and those assumptions spontane-
> ously issuing out of the state of thought respectively belonging
> to each of them. [1888, p. 364]

I have been positing, then, that representation is something created in the personality. I have brought forth as my proof the first
evidences of man in the civilized state as opposed to his barbarian

past, following them up with some comments from Damasio's neurophysiological research, a squint at Kant's philosophy, another at the thought of Maurice Blondel, then a look at Bion's psychological model of cognitive development, and, finally, a short excursion into the work of Newman. Each of these men came to a similar conclusion while studying human beings from different angles—Damasio currently from neurophysiological evidence, Bion recently from the evidence he gathered from the psychological phenomenology of psychotic patients, Kant at the turn of the eighteenth to nineteenth century from a desire to make coherent sense of the philosophically contradictory positions of the rationalists and the empiricists, Blondel in the tradition of Aristotle and the Scholastics at the end of the nineteenth century, and Newman stretching the length of the nineteenth century from his observations on the different conclusions arrived at by historians who were his contemporaries. I think that it would be wrong to conclude that the positions of these scholars, all working in different fields and at different times, came purely from the evidence that lay or lies in front of them. It is also their own personal construction of that evidence, guided, as Newman says, by what he called the "illative sense". However, it is apposite to put in a note about proof in the humanities.

Proof in the social sciences is of a different nature from that which we demand in physical science. In the latter we are able to find proof that can be measured. For instance, the Italian Camilo Golgi believed that neurons were joined together without any gap between them, but this was met with ferocious opposition from the Spanish anatomist Ramón y Cajal, who was convinced that there was a gap between neurons. The magnification of a light microscope was not sufficient to prove the matter either way, so both stuck to their point of view. However, with the invention of the electron microscope in the 1950s, it could be clearly seen that there is a gap between neurons—so Ramón y Cajal was right (Greenfield, 2003, pp. 91–95). In the field of astronomy Hubble was able to show that the galaxies are tearing away from us at tremendous speeds and that therefore the universe is expanding, which supports the Big Bang theory of the origin of the universe. The latter fits the facts and is generally accepted theory today among astronomers but is still open to different interpretations.

The object of scrutiny in the physical sciences are, therefore, particularities: proof here lies in observation and measurement. What decided the controversy between Golgi and Ramón y Cajal was the more accurate observation made possible through the invention of the electron microscope. Proof in the humanities or the social sciences is of a different kind: here we need to distinguish between certainty and dogmatism.

The object of scrutiny in the humanities has its foundation in the apprehension of reality itself, not essentially in any particular. So, for instance, Descartes came down to an elemental nonreducible certainty about his own existence through his own most inner generative activity. There has been much criticism of Descartes for settling upon thinking as the ultimate activity that then proves his own existence to himself. The social sciences are concerned to establish certainties about human beings in their essential inner nature. Thinking is a created reality, and it is through this creative activity of which thinking is a product, that human beings know themselves to exist. When we go to Altamira and look at the cave paintings, we know that these were made by humans like ourselves, not by cave-dwelling monkeys. We know this for certain. Certainty, then, is a consequence of creative activity. I will go further and say that certainty is a component of the creative act.

Now that which is created comes from an activity within the psyche, but it has an existence independent of it. Those paintings on the ceiling of Altamira have an existence that is independent of the people who painted them. Before they were painted, they had an independent existence within the mind, a mode of existing outside the self. Yet that created existence corresponds to what is already there. Let me give an example.

It was a creative act when Isaac Newton formulated the law of gravity, and yet it corresponded to what was already there; so we have this apparent contradiction that the reality was created but was also already there. This is an example of a form within physical science, but there are also forms existing between human beings—forms that are created yet are realities that are already present. There are certain forms within and between human beings that are present but require each individual to create. Now, in order to outline one of the most primordial forms, one that is so inherent that we hardly notice it, I am going to give you a clinical account that I hope will illustrate it:

I was treating a young woman who complained of the way which her boss at work treated her. I shall call her boss Mr Jones, and let her name be Mary. Her working hours were, for instance from nine in the morning until five in the evening, but this boss, Mr Jones, would frequently keep her back until half past six without any apology and without extra pay. He was offhand with her, he would not bother to listen to any requests that she made, and so on. He sounded in every way insensitive and exploitative. That was the reality. But was it? Now I'll introduce you to the next episode in my story.

I noticed that when I spoke to Mary, she didn't listen to what I said. I would speak, and she would continue talking as if I had not said anything. I pointed this out to her on several occasions, but it did not seem to have any visible effect. When I spoke, she ignored me; when I damaged my knee and hobbled round on a walking-stick, she ignored the fact—I did not seem to be present in her emotional landscape. As far as I could see, she behaved towards me in a way that was pretty similar to the way Mr Jones was behaving towards her.

One day I pointed out all the various ways in which she ignored me, and I drew a picture for her of an interconnecting pattern of attitudes towards me, but with more emphasis and conviction than before. Now, for the first time, I noticed that she paused, and I had the distinct impression that whereas before she had brushed all that I had said aside, this time she received it. After quite a long pause she said, in a rather tight manner: *"I can see what you mean."* For the rest of the session she spoke in a subdued manner.

That was a Tuesday morning. Now I'll tell you the next scene of this drama which was the Wednesday morning. She came in looking bright and cheerful, and she said:

"You know, something very curious happened yesterday. When I got to work, Mr Jones smiled at me. When the lunch hour came, he told me to make sure that I gave myself enough time for lunch. And at five o'clock, when he was in the middle of dictating letters, he looked at his watch and said, 'oh, it's time we broke off now and went home. I can give you the rest of these letters tomorrow'."

I was amazed at the time but this incident is no surprise to me today, because I have witnessed similar occurrences on numerous occasions. What I want to do is to attempt to understand psychologically what has happened, but this is itself a prelude to understanding one of the prime principles within the human sciences. How is it that Mr Jones's behaviour changed, and what connection is there between that and what I had said to Mary the previous day?

My first step is to presuppose that what occurred between Mary and Mr Jones was a consequence of what had occurred between her and me. When I spoke to her on that Tuesday morning and she gave the appearance of hearing me and receiving emotionally what I said, this affected the way Mr Jones behaved towards her later that morning. I conclude that the emotional occurrence in the session gave rise to her new relationship to Mr Jones later that day.

What happened between Mary and me was simple and yet deep. When I spoke to her with a new definiteness, she took in—received into herself—her own Mr Jones' mode of behaving. She was behaving this way towards me, but I think it is clear that she was behaving this way not only towards me, but towards others as well. There was, then, something true of her that she had disowned, that she refused to accept as part of her. Sometimes this is referred to in psychoanalytic terms as something *split off*. The way I have put it here is that until that Tuesday morning it had been disowned, but on that auspicious morning she *embraced* it. So we have here a formulation: that there are two states that an individual can be in: either one in which she disowns something that is her or one in which she embraces what is her; these two states are very different, and the human community judges them as different. Now to the next episode in our account.

Two weeks later, Mary said,

"You know, I don't think Mr Jones is as I thought him to be. I don't really think he is like that."

Then she went on to say,

> "The way he has been behaving towards me is how he really
> is. That is the real Mr Jones."

This seems to me to be a very important statement. Mary is dis-
tinguishing between *real* and *unreal*. But of course we know that
this does not refer to a judgement about whether Mr Jones exists
or not: that when she says he is *real*, she does not mean that he
exists, and when she says or implies that he is *unreal*, she means
he does not exist.

It begins to be clear, then, that when she says that Mr Jones is
real as opposed to *unreal*, it is not a statement about physical reality: it is an ethical statement. I deliberately use the term "ethical
statement" rather than the more usual sociological term "value
judgement" because it seems that not just Mary in the example
given, but, rather, we, whenever we use terms of someone such as
"genuine" as opposed to "fake", "true" as opposed to "false", we
are implying that there is one way of being that we endow with
terms like "real", "true", or "genuine" and another way that we
name "unreal", "false", or "fake": the difference lies in whether
someone has embraced all aspects of herself or not. When the
important aspects of the self have been embraced, then we use
terms like "real", "true", or "genuine"; when they have not been
embraced but disowned and, as revealed by Freud's researches,
in fact actively denied or hated, then we use words like "unreal",
"false", or "fake". It is further clear that to embrace oneself has
been judged by society as the better way to be. Therefore an ethical
proposition lies at the heart of the human or social sciences.

There is another important aspect to this. When I embrace parts
of myself within, it is part of an activity within the personality that
also governs the way I relate to the world outside, particularly the
human world. So with Mary it affected the way she related to Mr
Jones, which was reflected in the way he responded to her. That
inner embrace then characterizes the way the outer is perceived.
The inner emotional activity guides the way our perceptual system
operates. It is rather like the lens of a camera, which, depending on
its position, determines how the outer object is seen. When I talk
of the character of this inner embracing activity, I mean also that it

is a creative act. Like Newton's creative act of something that was already there, Mary created a reality that was already there.

I need to go back to that crucial intervention of mine. What I was doing was making a complaint to her about her way of relating to me. *"You ignore me"*, I was saying, *"You carry on as if I did not exist"*. Now I think there was a crucial element in the way that I did that which made it possible for her to receive it. There are two modes in which it is possible for me to say this. I am either in the role of the injured invalid or in the role of the scientist. I will dramatize the difference between the two. First, the injured invalid: Crying *"You horrible beast . . ."*, crying and snivelling, *"I do exist, you know. The way you treat me is unfair and horrible"*, snivel, snivel. Thus speaks the injured invalid. Now let us listen to the scientist. *"Now apart from yourself there is another person in this room. This other person is a fellow called Neville, but I think you do not know it. Think back to your first day at school when you did not know your two-times table. You did not know that two and two make four. They did make four, but you did not know it. There is this other fellow in this room, but I don't think you know it yet."* Then the scientist goes on to say that evidence for this is that Mary pushes away any interventions from Neville.

My point is that Mary is able to accept the intervention because it came sufficiently from the scientist. I say "sufficiently" because I would not want to claim that the injured invalid was totally out of the room, but his presence was considerably less than that of the scientist.

So the point is this that when emotional activities are scientifically observed, they are capable of being created. Just as Newton observed the connecting bonds between the movements of the planets in the solar system and created gravity, so Mary took those activities that I pointed out—activities that were aimed towards me but were a sample of uncreated activity within her—and created them into a personal form. So my conclusion to this is: that the communication and inner representation are both products of an inner creative activity.

There is another important point about that intervention of mine on that Tuesday morning. It was that I spoke with emotional certainty. Until then, when I had pointed out her ignoring of me, it came from the surface of me, it was said in reaction to what she was saying, whereas on that Tuesday morning it came from a different place in me. I had taken the surface statements and taken them into myself and gathered them there into the centre of myself. In simple language I spoke with certainty. It is very important to distinguish this from dogmatism. Certainty arises from the knowledge that I have created something at the centre of myself, but, like Newton, I have created something that is already there. Dogmatism is when I have ingested something said to me from outside myself and have allowed my own creative centre to be crushed under it. It means that one statement comes from the heart of the analyst or therapist, whereas the other is from a paralysed corpse. The words may be the same, but the emotional states that generate the same two statements are profoundly different. Going back to what we emphasized in chapter 2, the emotional state—the emotional activity—is the unit of communication, and it is this that will determine the responsive changes in the other.

"Certainty" is the name we give to a state of mind that arises from a unified inner coherence. On that propitious Tuesday morning Mary, my patient, met a new analyst. She was in relation to a different person. Thinking back to chapter 2, I might say that this carbon atom was in relation not to other carbon atoms as in a diamond but to a different atom as in an enzyme (Birch, 1995, p. 79). Her internal constitution had to take this new relation into consideration. The analyst had changed from being an aggregate into a unified being. He looked the same, sounded similar, and yet was a different being. She had to take this new being into inner consideration. It was not the words that I spoke that led to the change in her but my own emotional constitution, which her own inner world had to take account of. That moment of certainty had been preceded by that consistent staring, looking, and absorbing of the sensuous realities that I described in chapter 4 as being always the necessary predisposing attitude prior to that mysterious inner creative unification of the personality. The point I want to stress, however, is that it is this and not the words spoken that is the decisive factor that leads to change.

It is also this state that led Mary to refer to the post-Tuesday Mr Jones as the *real* Mr Jones. In other words, in the social sciences as opposed to the physical sciences a judgement is made that unified inner coherence is what is real and unreal is that which is in aggregate mode. Society ultimately has judged the former to be sane and the latter crazy.

So the conclusion is that there is a something within the personality. Blondel called it a *nothing*, Bion *alpha function*, Newman *the illative sense*. It is this lies at the heart of sanity, at the heart of civilization. So it is this that needs the most tender care.

CHAPTER SIX

The case of pseudo-maturity

The question: *How is it that someone who has a problem is able to resolve it through conversation with another?*

"The pinnacle of human development is attained when the inwardness of the individual guides and shapes his perceptions and controls his actions at every moment."

Wilhelm Dilthey [1989, pp. 287–288]

We have, I believe, tied up everything very neatly. Through conversation with another, the one who is suffering and creates suffering for others is able to form images through which she is able actively to embrace the hated elements within. When these have been embraced, they change their nature. Through communication with another, these elements pass through the transforming dynamo within. This is, as it were, given a charge, enabling it to do its job. So there we have it. I am full of distress, and in that state I go to visit my psychotherapist. Through intimate communication, my power of generating transforming images is renewed and enhanced. So I leave my psychotherapist and now all is well—or is it?

My instinct tells me that this is too neat. The contents of the parcel have been wrapped up too well. We have been so keen to create a neat parcel, so intense is my obsessional passion, that I have left out a few objects that are difficult to fit into my nicely folded paper. After all, a sharp object might puncture it and destroy all our work. So let us leave it there—or shall we? Let's be delinquent, let's be awkward. There is something that does not fit. What is it?

I have so far referred to a person with a problem in a general sort of way, but different people have different problems—no two people have the same. One man's problem is that he flies into a temper whenever someone treats him with disrespect. In the local newsagents he is spoken to in a dismissive way, and he shouts angrily and storms out. He is there with his girlfriend, who says that if he behaves like that once more, she will end the relationship. This brings him by a winding pathway to the psychotherapist's office. Another man comes because he had always been filled with passion and curiosity about life, but he notices that this has slowly diminished since his mother died two years ago. A woman had been going to work each day as a reporter on a fashion magazine when, looking out of the window of the high-rise office, she has a sudden impulse to throw herself to destruction onto the street twelve floors below. She arrives in panic, no longer able to trust that she can go to work and return home in the evening alive and not in a coffin. Another woman arrives at the age of 30 because she has never had a boyfriend and, although she has a full-packed life, she feels that she is "missing out". Another man is near retirement, and the thought of living out his days playing golf during the day and bridge in the evening catapults him into a dark cloud of desolation. Another woman comes because a psychiatrist has declared her to be suffering from OCD (obsessive-compulsive disorder) and wants to put her on antidepressants, and she hates the idea of going on drugs and has heard of a strange man who claims to heal "through talking". I can see a long queue of people outside the consulting-room door, each with their own very particular brand of suffering. Before leaving this suffering, I want to differentiate between each person's own source of suffering and the official version of madness according to the psychiatrist's textbook.

What I am pointing at is the difference between the individual's own definition of his problem and the official declaration of it. The examples I have just given are all of an individual nature. Each person arrives with a problem that is particular to him. The psychiatrist classifies problems according to a series of diseases. We all know their names: schizophrenia, manic-depressive psychosis, which is today called a bipolar disorder, hysteria, obsessional neurosis, psychopathy, borderline conditions, autism, Asperger's syndrome, and a huge host of new ones like RSI (repetitive strain injury), ADD (attention deficit disorder), ADHD (attention deficit hyperactivity disorder), and so on. What all these share is a definition that , at bottom, is based upon a condition that is a trouble to others. It is very important to realize this, because it conditions the mental outlook of the psychoanalyst or psychotherapist. I need to go into this a bit more clearly.

When I am mad, I do not know it. That is part of the definition of madness. Just as the definition of a bachelor is a man who is not married, so the definition of madness is that when I am in it I do not know it. You might bring forth instances of people who have known they are mad yet they do not know it while they are in it but only afterwards. I can be gripped by a fit of madness. I do not know it while I am in it, but I can know it a minute later, an hour later, a week later, a year later, or a decade later, but not while I am in it. The moment I know it, I cease to be mad.

A declaration of my own madness is always a thing of the past. So madness is a definition of myself in the past or of another person in the present. Society has defined madness as behaviour that is noxious to those around and of which the subject is not himself aware. Society is able, in grave circumstances, to incarcerate someone forcibly. This is because that person is a danger to themselves and other people. So society takes responsibility for the mad person. The different varieties of madness I have mentioned are based on the analogy of physical diseases.

It is an historical accident that distress of mind came under the charge of doctors. In the Middle Ages they were the responsibility of the Church. The history of this change is interesting enough; I have neither the competence nor the time to go into it, but I want instead to reflect for a moment on the fact that we understand mental realities always through an analogy. Let us speak even more simply. A mental reality is not seen in itself but only the effects of it, so we grasp it through an image. Let me give you an example. The philosopher Wittgenstein read one day in a newspaper of a man who was summoned to court on account of an accident while he was driving. In order to explain clearly to the judge exactly what had happened, he took into the courtroom with him a board—like a drafts or chess board—on which he had painted the roads, and then he had little models of his and the other cars, and he moved them, like a child playing a game, so the judge could see what had occurred. When Wittgenstein read this, he thought this was a very good image of how language imitates reality, and he explained his first theory of language based on that quaint imagery. The other example comes from Wilfred Bion, who said that "If a patient says he cannot take something in, or the analyst feels he cannot take something in, he implies a container and something to put in it" (1963/1989, pp. 6–7).

Therefore the relation of one reality to another is imaged as one thing being contained within another. Both Wittgenstein and Bion are using an image through which to grasp the relation between two mental realities. We can only ever grasp a mental reality through a picture of this kind. The picture used to describe madness prior to our modern era was a religious one. Madness was the consequence of sin. A man had spat in the face of God, and his maker struck back at him with madness. This was the mediaeval picture of madness. There were two images in this Mediaeval mythology: one was of the individual human being refusing the gift of God's love as offered to him or her through Christ, the other was that the human condition as a whole, with death, wars, disease, and suffering, was the consequence of the whole human race having spat in the face of God and been cast out of the Garden of Eden. This refusal of the gift of life was seen to lie at the heart of madness. Madness was a repudiation of what it was to be human. Madness was, in fact, something that deprived someone of their reasoning mind, and it was this that raised mankind onto a higher plane than the rest of the animal kingdom.

The picture of madness adopted by doctors was founded on the image of a physical disease, and this became elaborated most clearly by Kraepelin in the last quarter of the nineteenth century. Of course no image is perfect. Each has its restrictions. What are the advantages and the disadvantages of these two different images? The advantage of the Mediaeval picture is that there is inherently in it the idea that madness is something about which something can—and, indeed, should—be done. So if I have done something to bring about my madness, then logically I can do something to reverse the process. The converse side of it is that it can be extremely persecuting for me to believe that my madness is all due to my own culpable sinfulness. In fact, the idea of a God who accuses me for my sinfulness lies at the heart of the mad condition. The lunatic screaming in the lonesome night at the moon's magnetizing light captures in essence what drives the suffering creature into madness (see Pirandello's short story, "Mal di luna" [Moon sickness]). God scrutinizing the depths of my soul with a bright light is what drives me mad. Compared to this, the image of madness as a disease seems a welcome relief. A doctor comes and ministers to the one who is ill. However, I think that what we have is something that has combined these two images: that is, a disease that has accreted to itself God's accusing finger. The idea of a physical illness is free of any such accusation, and so we might think that Kraepelin had done us all a service in classifying the condition of madness within the catalogue of disease entities. But I think we all know how these conditions still tend to accrete to themselves an accusing tone. "He is very narcissistic"; "he's a bit schizoid"; "she's a flagrant hysteric": the tone is critical, and the inference is that it is his or her fault.

There is another image that has arisen since the last quarter of the nineteenth century. It is that madness is due to trauma in childhood—in particular, it has come about through neglectful mothering or, to quote the modern jargon, neglect from the infant's primary caregiver. However, this also has become tinged with God's accusing finger. The difference is that the finger is pointing now at the mother or early caregivers, rather than at the mad person himself. So this new imagery does not free us from this accusing taint.

I think that a difficult mental job has to be done in order to lay a new foundation: one that exchanges God for fate. I am going to summarize something that appears in chapter 5 of an infamous book called *A Pattern of Madness*. The question the author asks is:

"How does the perspective that gives rise to madness become reversed so that we no longer have madness but sanity?"

If we can answer this question, we shall have made a momentous contribution. The problem is that the answer is something that each individual clinician has to make, and what is more, we are not talking of an intellectual answer alone but one that is intellectual *and* emotional—or, as I have preferred to call it here, "higher-order emotional". Therefore it requires not just an intellectual effort but an emotional transformation. What we are looking for, then, is a reversal of a perspective that generates madness. To do this, we have to banish a very basic belief that underpins our whole way of thinking in Western culture.

I can illustrate it best by giving a clinical example. A patient, called "Nadie", had had a traumatic childhood. Her mother had died giving birth to her, and she had then been brought up by her father's sister, but as a young child she had been told that this aunt was her mother. It was only later that she learned she was not her mother, and then she referred to her as "Aunty–Mumma". Now in adult life she illustrated two aspects of a godlike behaviour. She would castigate herself in the fiercest way, and she would tempt me, her therapist, to do the same. Also, she had damaged herself very severely, both financially and otherwise. She put all her inheritance into a most farcical investment, and she had partnered up with men who were extremely exploitative of her. The question is "Why?" It was also clear that she was broken up inside; she used to say, "I am all in bits". If she was in an agitated state one day, she would not remember anything about her agitation the following day. In a session she would make an angry retort to an interpretation; when I referred to this half a minute later, she would utterly deny the retort. It took me time to realize that she had forgotten it—so she was in bits, but also time was chopped up into bits, and one bit was unconnected to another: yesterday had no connection with today, and this morning had no connection with this afternoon. It seemed that this broken-up state of her psyche had a connection with this self-destructive behaviour and self-castigation. My proposition is that to have a god castigating her was preferable to being the casualty of a traumatic accident.

The best way of approaching this question is to start by quoting this passage from the Bible:

> And when they came to the threshing floor of Næcón, Uzzah put out his hand to the ark of God and took hold of it, for the

oxen stumbled. And the anger of the Lord was kindled against Uzzah; and God smote him there because he put forth his hand to the ark; and he died there beside the ark of God. And David was angry because the Lord had broken forth upon Uzzah; and that place is called Pê`rêz-ùz`æh to this day. [2 Samuel 6: 6–8]

Now the question is: "What has happened here?" This is the way I interpret it. The oxen cart carrying the Ark of the Covenant was coming down a rough mountain path; one of the two oxen stumbled, Uzzah rushed forward to try to steady it, but it fell and crushed him to death. In modern journalistic reporting the incident might go like this:

"At Nacon, twenty kilometres from Jerusalem, the oxen carrying the Ark of the Covenant to the Temple stumbled. A man rushed forward to steady the cart, but it toppled over and crushed him. He was rushed by ambulance to hospital but was dead on arrival. The man's name was Uzzah."

or even perhaps:

"At Nacon, twenty miles from Jerusalem, the truck carrying the Ark of the Covenant had a tyre burst, and it skidded and crashed into a bollard at the side of the road. The driver, Mr Uzzah, was killed . . ."

So why in the Bible is this incident attributed to God, to Yahweh? I think it is significant that David was angry with Yahweh. I believe it was attributed to Yahweh because that is easier to manage emotionally than is attributing it to sheer accident. Henri Bergson said that if a rock rolled down a hill and hit a stone-age man and killed him, he would attribute it to an evil spirit (1935, pp. 119ff); Freud makes a similar point in *The Future of an Illusion*:

There are elements, which seem to mock at all human control: the earth, which quakes and is torn apart and buries all human life and its works; water, which deluges and drowns everything in a turmoil; storms, which blow everything before them; there are diseases, which we have only recently recognized as attacks by other organisms; and finally there is the painful riddle of death, against which no medicine has yet been found, nor probably will be. With these forces nature rises up against us, majestic, cruel and inexorable; she brings to our mind once more our weakness and helplessness, which we thought to escape through the work of civilization . . .

Impersonal forces and destinies cannot be approached; they remain eternally remote. But if the elements have passions that rage as they do in our own souls, if death itself is not something spontaneous but the violent act of an evil Will, if everywhere in nature there are Beings around us of a kind that we know in our own society, then we can breathe freely, can feel at home in the uncanny and can deal by psychical means with our own senseless anxiety. We are still defenceless, perhaps, but we are no longer helplessly paralysed; we can at least react. Perhaps, indeed, we are not even defenceless. We can apply the same methods against these violent supermen outside that we employ in our own society; we can try to adjure them, to appease them, to bribe them, and, by so influencing them, we may rob them of a part of their power. [1927c, pp. 15–17]

So god is fashioned to protect us from the senselessness of an accident. A trauma is an accidental happening—something that the individual was incapable of avoiding or preventing. It may have been something that happened in childhood. Nadie's mother died giving birth to her, and many unfortunate consequences followed from that. Neither the disaster of her mother's death nor the consequences could have been prevented by Nadie. And this trauma breaks the spirit. It breaks the human psyche into those bits that I have named the "narcissistic constellation", of which god is a part. It is an animistic way of talking to say that it is the god in the personality that obliterates pain and self-destructiveness or that propels hated elements into the body or surrounding figures. That such obliteration and propulsion takes place is accurate, but to call god the agent is the same as the Biblical author saying that Yahweh struck down Uzzah. The agent of the obliteration and propulsion is the scattered "bits-in-the-jelly". We call it "god" because it looks to the observer like grandiosity, or it feels to the subject like a godlike authority subjecting him or her to a fierce castigation. What I am saying here is that this definition arises from the subjective experience of the other, even if "the other" is the recipient in one's own self. This means that interpretations about the patient's omnipotence are psychologically incorrect.

The conversion of "an accident" into intentionality is the source of masochism. The authoritarian voice in the personality condemns and tells the individual that this is all his fault or that she is to blame, or it may be turned around and the voice says that the mother was to blame. In both cases it is an attempt at a simplistic explanation. To avoid that explanation and see it as a nameless accident requires the human being to stretch his mind and to embrace a metaphysical dimension. It is very common for a clinician to point out some limitation to a patient, and then the patient adds to what has been said:

> *"Yes, I am always very bad at listening to people. Often I don't bother, and frequently I just indulge my own thoughts . . ."*
>
> *"Yes, I know it is not only my brother I put down. When I am teaching, I often put down my pupils quite unnecessarily . . ."*
>
> *"I am just a rotten bastard. I don't deserve to be trusted in people's company at all . . ."*

It is preferable to think in this way. There is some sense that it is under control rather than uncontrolled activity flowing from "bits-in-the-jelly", from an accidental disaster.

An understanding that even the most perverse, mad, or psychopathic behaviour is the existence of the trauma in transformed mode is the clinician's foundation stone. A patient comes to a clinician in the hope that he can get help for this state of affairs. If help is available, then it must lie in the communication between the clinician and the afflicted individual. How it is that communication is curative is what we must now try to understand.

What we are saying here is that there needs to be a complete re-making of what has been established. To do this, the patient first needs to break down the building she has made and start again. It is deconstructing a personality that is pseudo-mature and re-fashioning it into one that is truly mature. I will start with an example.

Anna was brought up in a small village called Sinai in New Hampshire on the eastern seaboard of the United States. Her grandfather had migrated to the States from southern Italy and had fathered 12 children. His wife came of New England stock and had all the religious intensity that is familiar to us through Arthur

Miller's play, *The Crucible*. All the children were brought up in the strictest fashion, and the eldest boy, Raphael, married Louisa, who was also from another strictly religious New England family. Raphael and Louisa had five children—a girl, three boys, and a girl. Anna was this youngest girl, and she was almost adopted by her elder sister, Sarah. Her own mother, burdened with household chores and duties to the parish in which she lived, was content for Anna to be mothered by Sarah. Anna was like Cinderella. When Sarah was going out to a party, Anna helped her into her dress, pinned the pleats of her blouse, and felt happy and rewarded to see Sarah going off looking beautiful and giving Anna a fond kiss before she went. At one of these parties Sarah met a young man, Rowan, who proposed to her. Rowan was in fact Australian and was in New England visiting relatives so, once the marriage had been solemnized, he returned with Sarah to Sydney. Poor Anna was distraught. She moped and tramped around the house in misery. Then she received a letter from Sarah. She was going to have a baby. Would Anna come and help Sarah when the baby was to be born? Anna leapt for joy and in a short time she left for Sydney in time for the birth of Sarah's baby. So she became Sarah's helpmate, and, repeating a pattern already established back in the States in the family home, she would help Sarah get dressed in the evenings when she was going out with Rowan. She would be delighted to see Sarah in a white chiffon dress accompanying her husband while she stayed and looked after Lucia, the adored baby. Once or twice young men asked her out, but, even though she was sweet and attractive, no man ever asked her out a second time. The third time this happened, Anna became glum and dejected. She got up late in the morning, forgot to feed Lucia, and burnt the potatoes that she was frying for the evening meal. Sarah thought it was a passing mood, but when it went on day after day and week after week, she fumed at Anna:

"You're becoming lazy. You need to pull yourself together."

and:

"You're no use to me when you are behaving like this."

and:

"You'll have to go back home to Sinai if you can't be of help to me."

Three days after this, Anna did not come down to breakfast. Sarah went upstairs to her bedroom. Anna was in a comatose state. She had taken an overdose of sleeping tablets. Sarah called Rowan, who rushed her in his car to Prince Alfred Hospital. In the psychiatric unit she was pumped out and, after being seen by a psychiatrist, was referred for treatment to a psychotherapist: Agnes Shuttlehen enters the stage again.

In all her career as a psychotherapist, Agnes had never come across a patient who was so polite and obliging. Anna arrived at nine in the morning. She asked Agnes how she was, whether she had had a good week, and sent Agnes an angelic smile. Agnes felt annoyed, but, because she had trained herself to monitor her countertransference, she digested her annoyance. Why was Anna behaving in this way? she asked herself. It also became clear to Agnes that Anna believed that Agnes had no interest in her what-ever, and, although she was paying Agnes for her sessions and therefore one might think she would feel entitled to expect some-thing from Agnes, her whole way of conceiving things was quite different. She believed that she was there to serve Agnes and do her bidding.

Then one day Anna broke her leg. She was rushing to catch a bus to visit Agnes, and she tripped. Agnes decided to visit her for her session each week at the hospital. This amazed Anna. It gave her belief system a seismic shock. Perhaps she was worth some-thing in her own right. The little 5% sent shock waves through the 95%.

When five weeks later Anna returned home, Sarah discovered a very different sister from the one she had been used to. She de-clared that she wanted to be paid for looking after Lucia, that she was going to enrol at Sydney University to study psychology, and that she was going to go out on Friday nights and would in future only baby-sit on Wednesday and Saturday evenings. She did not deliver this information to Sarah in a quiet rational talk, but these were the outcomes of several explosive rows. The first was when Sarah assumed that Anna would look after Lucia on a Friday evening and was furious when she only arrived back at home an hour after the time that Sarah and Rowan had planned to go out. After shouting at each other, Anna declared that Friday nights were for her, and that Sarah never thought of her. Then on another occasion Sarah expected Anna to look after Lucia all day while she went to a conference; Anna broke out again in fury, and in the interchange she announced that she was going to enrol at Sydney University to study psychology. So little Anna, meek and mild, had become ragingly paranoid. Agnes was an experienced psychotherapist who stayed quiet and observed what was occurring. She realized that the 5% seedling was bursting forth in fury at her erstwhile oppressors. It was too violent to be calmly transformed into safe internal imagery. Events can only be converted into imagery when they are below a certain threshold of turbulence. The artist with his canvas trying to paint a seascape cannot do so when there is a hurricane blowing over his easel and spraying sand onto the paints on his palette. Only when the wind has died down can he set about converting what he has seen onto the canvas.

What we see in Anna is a transformation from pseudo-personality to genuine. There is a particular problem when the pseudo-personality is far removed from who the person really is. The pseudo-structure has to be broken down first. Storm Jameson, in her novel, *The Road from the Monument* (1962), describes Gregory Mott, her central character, as a man who has become famous as the Director of the Rutley Institute of Arts. He has a hand-written letter from Churchill and is to preside over an International Conference for artists and writers. While they are in Nice on holiday, his wife becomes ill, so he goes to a restaurant and has dinner on his own. He notices a young English girl not being able to pay for her meal, having left her purse at her hotel. He goes over to her, helps her out, has coffee with her, returns to her hotel, sleeps with her and . . . three months later receives the news that she is pregnant. By steady steps of predictable inevitability his grand role and reputation decompose. His friends (I would prefer to call them doubtful allies) cannot understand why he slept with that young woman in Nice. I think, though, the reason is that decomposition has to happen before there can be a rebuilding.

Both these examples are fictitious, but like all good fiction, they correspond to life as we meet it. In both these cases the misdemeanours—in the one case the overdose and in the other the adultery—happen under impulse. There is no sense in either of these two characters that they are at the start of constructing a new personality for themselves. Probably the answer is that the false cloak they have been wearing is made of imprisoning steel, and they cannot but throw it off in a fit of unpremeditated passion. However, there are cases—rarer, I think—where the person with the false armour has a vague sense that what he is wearing does not really fit him as he is, or that something is changing and requires a new suit of clothing. However, if there is a huge disjunction between who he is and the personality he has fashioned for himself, then again a representation cannot just equably happen in the quiet dialogue between psychoanalyst and patient.

So what is this example designed to illustrate? I started by saying that the picture I had drawn was too neat—too neat because there was an assumption in it that all could be converted into inner imagery within the dialogue going on between analyst and patient. But it seems that something can only be converted directly into inner imagery if there is no hatred. When there is intense hatred, more powerful than any love that is present, then this benign conversion cannot occur, or at least it cannot occur directly. If there is a vague awareness, then a person can decide to engage in a conscious piece of work that functions as a necessary preface to the job of representation. The representation cannot happen until this groundwork has been done. Why? Representation, if it is to be genuine, is an activity of the whole person. It has, therefore, to be a representation of *something*, and that *something* has first to be fashioned, and it has first to be expelled out of the personality. Anna hates being in that subservient position: it is the activities in her that enslave her that she hates. There is a violent rebellion against this enslaving activity of hers. She siphons out the attitude, separating the self-killing element out of the compound, which then manifests itself in the action of taking an overdose. It is separated out so that the rest of the personality can be spared its poisoning putrefaction. Then and only then can the work of reconstruction begin. So was the overdose a good or a bad thing? I cannot help here quoting a stanza from Andrew Marvell's poem *The Definition of Love*:

Magnanimous Despair alone
Could show me so divine a thing
Where feeble Hope could ne'er have flown
But merely flapped its tinsel wing.

[Marvell, 1986, p. 49]

There are two axes we have to consider here. The first is the practical one: if it had killed Anna, it would have been difficult to think that it was a good thing. If she survived, then we move to the second axis. What is the emotional attitude of the carers? If her overdose is viewed simply as an act of self-harm, then a protective and probably patronizing emotional posture comes into play. If, on the other hand, through a severe effort of thought and observation, it is met with humble respect for someone daring to rebuild her life from a new and effective foundation, then this embryo receives a great surge of new life. The emotional attitude of the carers has a potent effect upon the outcome of this new turn of events. If it is pitying, then the new plant will be stunted; if it is respectful, it will bloom with new vigour.

In the case of Gregory Mott, what is hated is his grandiosity. In the novel it is hated by Penny, the wife of his best friend, Tony Lambert, but I believe that this represents his own hatred of it. Why? Because it robs him of freedom. The grandiosity forces him to adopt many status roles that imprison him and stifle the inner creative centre of his being. This, I believe, is why he sleeps with the girl. This is the motive force that none of his friends can understand. Why on earth should he have done so foolish a thing? The grandiosity has to be deflated before he can make a vital contact with his own person.

So, I suspect, there is little awareness in the case of Gregory Mott, and only slightly more in the case of Anna. But I want now to turn to those rarer cases of people who have a larger percentage of awareness. In that case, the event that shakes up the personality does not come unsought, unsent: it is sought out with intention. In this case the individual knows that he has to *do* something *with* himself before he can bring that something into the frame of a representation. I think in this case three factors are interconnected: (1) intensity, (2) that it is woven into the texture of the personality, and (3) that this is hated.

When something is extremely intense, it cannot be gathered into the coherence necessary to make it into a picture. In the formulation of Wilfred Bion it exists in an array of unformed particles, which he calls "beta elements". I will give you an example of this. Mariana, a violent woman, had been brought up very largely by an elder sister, Ida, who was 17 years older than herself. I say she was violent because she told me in her initial interview that in a jealous rage with one boyfriend she had thrown all the furniture of his fourth-floor flat out of the window onto the street far below, and with another she had driven his car at speed into a tree at the side of the road. Her suppressed rage was palpable as she came into the room each day. When she started in analysis, she had not seen her sister for several years, and then only occasionally. When the analysis started, Mariana began visiting her sister regularly. Each time she went, she had a childlike hope that she would be given a warm welcome, but each time Ida treated her with casualness—one time forgetting altogether that her sister was coming, on another occasion she was asleep when Mariana arrived, and so on. At this time I was a novice in the art of psychoanalysis, and I kept wondering why on earth she kept visiting when each time she was knocked back by her sister. I knew it had something to do with the analysis, because these visits to her sister started contemporaneously with the beginning of the analysis. What I did not realize at the time was that Mariana was intentionally exposing herself to these repeated disappointments. Then one day she had this dream:

> I was at Ida's house, and she came into the room, and I picked up a knife and stabbed her in the chest and ripped open her rib-cage and blood poured out . . .

She was shocked, but I think this is what was happening. There was a huge rage inside against her sister who had treated her negligently, and this had been inside her since childhood, so, with studied consideration, Mariana went visiting her sister to re-awaken in herself the intense rage against her sister for being so uncaring of her in her childhood. I think that by reawakening it and, at the same time, diluting some of its intensity though displacing part of its passion onto me, she was able to form a representation of it, and that dream was the start of representation. I doubt that it could have happened, had she not entered in the experience of her disappointment with her sister. I think it would be a grave error to think that these renewed visits to her sister were in some way an avoidance of the work of the analysis. So this example is designed to show why it is that a very intense emotion has first to be entered into in a practical bodily way.

A woman called Christina was very cultured and refined, and she allowed people to exploit her not only in her work, but also in her relations with men. It was part of her personality—or so it seemed. Her family and friends knew her as extremely courteous. She came for analysis because she had been sitting on a terrace by the sea when she suddenly felt a chasm open up under her feet, and she sank into it and disappeared completely. This vision was transitory, but it kept coming back, and it frightened her. This indicated to the analyst that her own personhood was buried, and, as time proceeded, he guessed that it was buried under a politeness that had become not just a style but an addictive passion.

One day Christina revealed that she found great pleasure in encouraging her boyfriend to stand over her and piss upon her body. I made a connection in my mind between her allowing herself to be exploited, which seemed so inherent a part of her character, and her need to have her boyfriend piss upon her. It also seemed that this had begun to develop after her analysis had started. She believed that she needed to do it. I also thought that this was probably true, though I could not at that time have told you why or what its purpose was. I was sure, though, that it was connected to her submissiveness, which allowed her to be exploited both in her business ventures and in her love life and social life. I think, however, that what was happening was that she was beginning to separate that submissive part of her characterological behaviour that was intertwined into the fabric of her personality from her core self. This sexual behaviour continued for several years, and it was significant that she frequently talked of it; she used to say, "I know I need to talk about it". Then the attraction of it began to diminish, and she started to reveal herself more fully to me. I had not known before that she wrote poetry and was a keen botanist. I understood that her core self was now available and revealed because the submissive element had been siphoned out of her via the combination of the sexual activity, combined with reflective thought upon it. I don't think the representation could have occurred without her own engagement with that part of herself.

In both these cases the element that was seeking representation was, I think, also prevented through a hatred of it. In the case of Mariana, it was a hatred of her imprisoning mode of attachment;

with Christina, it was of the submissive element woven into the fabric of her being. They were hated because they smothered the creative core and severely restricted their freedom. So in both cases the restricting element had to be viewed with love or at least benign acceptance. When this had happened, representation could occur. It is, I think, a safe principle that we cannot be whole persons unless all parts of us have been gathered inside us, as a hen gathers all her eggs into contact with her warm, feathery body. If there has been hatred, the individual needs to enter into relation in a vital, engaged way before representation can happen. Just as primitive hatred is a banishment *in action* of elements within the personality, so primitive love is entering into those elements *in action*. When they have been entered into through behavioural deeds, then they can be represented. Why is this? I think it is that before they can be pictured, they first have to be touched. When a blind man is given back his sight through an operation, at first he cannot see what is in front of him. He has to touch the object before he can see it. I think it is the same with an element in the personality—it first has to be touched, and only then can it be seen. Two litters of kittens were born at the same time. One litter were allowed to scramble around in normal feline mode, the other was kept in a basket so that their feet were not in contact with the world around. When their eyes opened after ten days, the former were able to see, but the latter could not because they had not touched the world around. The tactile sense is the more basic: it does not have to be learned, whereas seeing does. We do not realize this because we learned it so early in our lives. But the same principle is at work here: if an element has not been seen, then it first has to be touched, and only then can it be "seen" or pictured.

What is clinically so important, therefore, is that the analyst does not in any way contribute to this hatred. So, for instance, let us look at the examples of Mariana and Christina. It would be a mistake for the analyst to point out to Mariana that she was denying what she knew of her sister, Ida's attitude towards her. Mariana needs to enter the experience, touch the experience.

I have had several patients who have told me in different ways that their parents had insisted that they learn from their parents' own experience and teaching, and they had held their children back from experiencing things themselves. This I always take to be a message telling me not to protect my patients from experiences that they need to enter into. There is one version of this that we commonly fall into. The patient says,

> *"Oh, I have just thought of something, but think you might disapprove . . ."*

and the analyst answers,

> *"What makes you think I shall disapprove?"*

thereby preventing the patient from entering the experience of being disapproved of. She needs to touch and feel what disapproval is like, but this reply has prevented it, because it effectively says,

> *"Don't worry, there will be no disapproval here . . ."*

This is one way an analyst stops the patient touching the experience. The point is this: the patient's psyche is deprived of the experience of disapproval, but the capacity to experience this is part of growing up into adulthood.

The other is when the analyst refers to something as greed, envy, jealousy, or omnipotence. They all sound bad and have the same deterrent effect. It is necessary that the analyst analyse what these elements are and describe them psychologically to the patient so they can be touched. To refer to something as greedy is a command saying:

> *"Don't touch."*

These are instances of interactions that occur directly between the patient and the analyst, but in the case of Mariana and Christina the activity is happening between the patient and someone outside the consulting-room. Here I believe it is imperative that the analyst does not interpret these activities as some form of "acting out". The very use of such a term suggests that the patient is endowed with a fully matured ego and could act differently if he wanted to. There is no understanding here that the patient is engaged in an initiatory courtship with the part of themselves that had, until then, been banished with hatred. Any statements about "acting out" and so on join with the terrorist hatred of that part of the personality.

So to sum up: there is a stage necessary between acceptance and representation that is the tactile phase, and the sense of this stage in the development is crucial. And so the central point of this book is that to represent, it is necessary for some people to first enter an experience. If this is bypassed, then the result may be pseudo-maturity rather than maturity.

REFERENCES

Anargyros-Klinger, A. (2002). *International Journal of Psychoanalysis, 83* (2: April).

Balkanyi, C. (1964). On verbalization. *International Journal of Psychoanalysis, 45*: 64–74.

Bergson, H. (1935). *The Two Sources of Morality and Religion.* London: Macmillan.

Berlin, I. (1979). *Against the Current.* London: Hogarth Press.

Bion, W. R. (1962/1984). *Learning from Experience.* London: William Heinemann Medical Books/Karnac.

Bion, W. R. (1963/1989). *Elements of Psychoanalysis.* London: William Heinemann Medical Books/Karnac.

Bion, W. R. (1970). *Attention and Interpretation.* London, Sydney, Toronto, Wellington: Tavistock Publications.

Bion, W. R. (1980). *Bion in New York and São Paulo.* Strath Tay: Clunie Press.

Bion, W. R. (1992). *Cogitations.* London: Karnac.

Birch, C. (1995). *Feelings.* Sydney: University of New South Wales Press.

Blake, W. (1972). *Blake—Complete Writings: Infant Sorrow—Songs of*

Experience. Oxford, New York, Toronto, Melbourne: Oxford University Press.

Blondel, M. (1984). *Action [1893].* Notre Dame, IN: University of Notre Dame Press.

Bryant, A. (1969). *The Lion and the Unicorn.* London: Collins.

Chaudhuri, H. (1987). *The Philosophy of Love.* London: Routledge & Kegan Paul.

Chesterton, G. K. (1910). *What's Wrong with the World.* London, New York, Toronto, Melbourne: Cassell.

Cicero (1984). Laelius: On friendship. In: *Cicero on the Good Life.* Harmondsworth, Middlesex: Penguin.

Coelho, P. (1996). *O Alquimista.* Cascais, Portugal: Editora Pergaminho.

Collingwood, R. G. (1969). *An Essay on Metaphysics.* Oxford: Clarendon Press.

Damasio, A. (1994). *Descartes' Error.* New York: Grosset/Putnam.

Damasio, A. (2000). *The Feeling of What Happens.* London: Vintage Books.

Damasio, A. (2003). *Looking for Spinoza.* London: William Heinemann.

de Gelder, B., Vroomen, J., Pourtois, G., & Weiskrantz, L. (1999). Nonconscious recognition of affect in the absence of striate cortex. *NeuroReport, 10*: 3759–3763.

Dennett, D. (1993). *Consciousness Explained.* Harmondsworth, Middlesex: Penguin.

Dilthey, W. (1989). The facts of consciousness (Breslau Draft). In: *Selected Works: Introduction to the Human Sciences.* Princeton, NJ: Princeton University Press.

Dostoyevsky, F. (1978). *Crime and Punishment.* Harmondsworth, Middlesex: Penguin.

Eliot, G. (1973). *Middlemarch.* Harmondsworth, Middlesex: Penguin.

Eucken, R. (1913). *The Life of the Spirit.* New York: G. P. Putnam's Sons; London: Williams & Norgate.

Field, J. [Marion Milner] (1987a). *An Experiment in Leisure.* Los Angeles: Jeremy P. Tarcher; New York: St. Martin's Press.

Field, J. [Marion Milner] (1987b). *A Life of One's Own.* London: Virago.

Fonagy, P., Steele, H., & Steele, M. (1991). Maternal representations of attachment during pregnancy predict the organisation of infant–mother attachment at one year of age. *Child Development, 62*: 891–905.

Freud, S. (1893f). Charcot. *S.E. 3.* London: Hogarth Press & The Institute of Psycho-Analysis.

Freud, S. (1913c). On the beginning of treatment. *S.E. 12.* London: Hogarth Press & The Institute of Psycho-Analysis.

Freud, S. (1914d). On the history of the psycho-analytic movement. *S.E. 14.* London: Hogarth Press & The Institute of Psycho-Analysis.

Freud, S. (1915e). The unconscious. *S.E. 14.* London: Hogarth Press & The Institute of Psycho-Analysis.

Freud, S. (1927c). *The Future of an Illusion. S.E. 21.* London: Hogarth Press & The Institute of Psycho-Analysis.

Fromm, E. (1972). *Psychoanalysis and Religion.* New York: Bantam Books; New Haven, CT: Yale University Press.

Garner, H. (1996). Killing Daniel. In: *True Stories*. Melbourne: Text Publishing.

Gombrich, E. H. (1974). *The Story of Art.* London: Phaidon Press.

Greenfield, S. (2003). *The Human Brain.* London: Weidenfeld & Nicolson–Phoenix Book.

Hausheer, R. (1979). Introduction. In: I. Berlin, *Against the Current*. London: Hogarth Press.

Hazlitt, W. (1908). The ignorance of the learned. In: *Table Talk or Original Essays. Everyman Library No 321.* London & Toronto: J. M. Dent & Sons.

Hobson, P. (1993). *Autism and the Development of Mind.* Hove, U.K., & Hillsdale, NJ: Lawrence Erlbaum.

Hobson, P. (2002). *The Cradle of Thought.* London: Macmillan.

Holmes, J. (1993). *John Bowlby and Attachment Theory.* London & New York: Routledge.

Houselander, C. (1952). *Guilt.* London: Sheed & Ward.

Hubel, D. H. (1988). *Eye, Brain and Vision.* New York: Scientific American Library.

Huxley, A. (1980). *The Perennial Philosophy*. London: Chatto & Windus.

James, W. (1989). *The Principles of Psychology.* Chicago, London, Toronto, Geneva, Sydney, Tokyo, Manila: William Benton.

Jameson, S. (1962). *The Road from the Monument*. London & New York: White Lion.

Jones, E. (1972). *Sigmund Freud: Life and Work, Vol. 1: The Young Freud*. London: Hogarth Press.

Jung Chang (1991). *Wild Swans: Three Daughters of China*. London: Simon & Schuster.

Kelley, C. F. (1977). *Meister Eckhart on Divine Knowledge*. New Haven, CT, & London: Yale University Press.

Kierkegaard, S. (1971). *Either/Or*. Princeton, NJ: Princeton University Press.

Koestler, A. (1969). *The Act of Creation*. London: Picador, Pan Books.

Lewis, C. S. (1987). *The Screwtape Letters*. London: Collins, Fount Paperbacks.

Lonergan, B. (1957). *Insight*. London: Darton, Longman & Todd.

Macmurray, J. (1935). *Reason and Emotion*. London: Faber & Faber.

Macmurray, J. (1991). *Persons in Relation*. Atlantic Highlands, NJ, & London: Humanities Press International.

Marvell, A. (1986). *The Complete Poems*. Harmondsworth, Middlesex: Penguin.

Newman, J. H. (1888). *An Essay in Aid of a Grammar of Assent*. London: Longmans, Green.

Newman, J. H. (1927). *The Idea of a University*. New York & London: Longmans, Green.

Scholem, G. (1995). *Major Trends in Jewish Mysticism*. New York: Schocken Books.

Symington, N. (2002a). Letter. *International Journal of Psychoanalysis, 83* (6, December).

Symington, N. (2002b). *A Pattern of Madness*. London: Karnac.

Symington, N. (2003a). Healing the mind: What is the process? *Australasian Journal of Psychotherapy, 22* (1): 11–22.

Symington, N. (2003b). Healing the mind: What is the healer's task? *Australasian Journal of Psychotherapy, 22* (1): 25–36.

Teilhard de Chardin, P. (1960). *The Phenomenon of Man*. London: Collins.

Turnbull, C. (1984). *The Forest People*. London: Triad/Paladin, Granada Publishing.

Tustin, F. (1972). *Autism and Child Psychosis*. London: Hogarth Press.

Tustin, F. (1986). *Autistic Barriers in Neurotic Patients*. London: Karnac.

Vuilleumier, P., & Schwartz, S. (2001a). Beware and be aware: Capture of spatial attention by fear-related stimuli in neglect. *NeuroReport,* *12*: 1119–1122.

Vuilleumier, P., & Schwartz, S. (2001b). Modulation of visual perception by eye gaze direction in patients with spatial neglect and extinction. *NeuroReport, 12*: 2101–2104.

Whitehead, A. N. (1942). *Adventure of Ideas.* Harmondsworth, Middlesex: Penguin.

Winnicott, D. (1965). *The Maturational Processes and the Facilitating Environment.* London: Hogarth Press & The Institute of Psycho-Analysis.

Zweig, S. (1939/1953). *Beware of Pity.* London, Toronto, Melbourne, Sydney, Wellington: Cassell.

INDEX